FEARLESSLY
UNSHACKLED

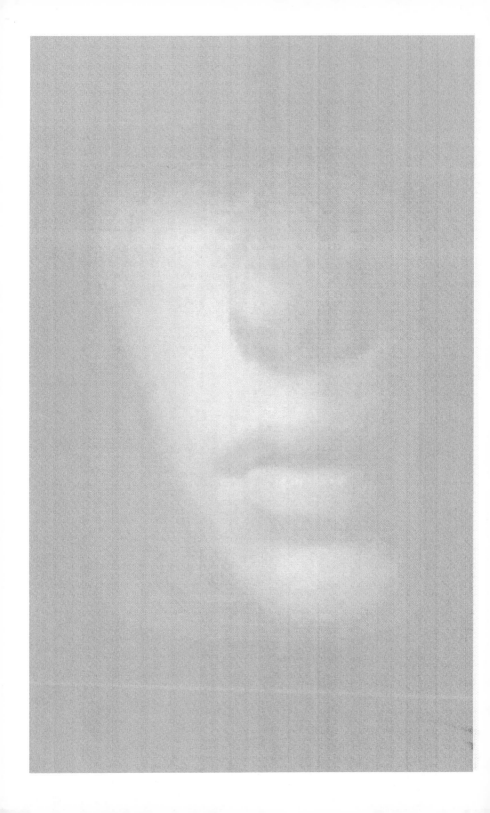

FEARLESSLY
UNSHACKLED

Breaking Free from the Voice of Destruction
into Your Purpose and Promise

SARAH ANN ROSE

Integrity Publishing
Augusta, Georgia

Published in Augusta, Georgia, by Integrity Publishing LLC. www.bookswithintegrity.com

Unless otherwise noted, Scripture quotations are taken from the Holy Bible, New International Version®, NIV®,Copyright © 1973, 1978, 1984, 2011 by Biblica, Inc.® Used by permission. All rights reserved worldwide.

Scripture quotations marked (AMP) are taken from the Amplified® Bible, Copyright © 2015 by The Lockman Foundation. Used by permission. www.Lockman.org

Scripture quotations marked (CSB) are taken from the Christian Standard Bible. Copyright © 2017 by Holman Bible Publishers. Used by permission. Christian Standard Bible®, and CSB® are federally registered trademarks of Holman Bible Publishers, all rights reserved.

Scripture quotations marked (ERV) are taken from the Easy-To-Read Version Copyright © 2006 by Bible League International. All rights reserved.

Scripture quotations marked (ESV®) are taken from The Holy Bible, English Standard Version®, Copyright © 2001 by Crossway, a publishing ministry of Good News Publishers. Used by permission. All rights reserved.

Scripture quotations marked (KJV) are taken from The King James Version which is public domain.

Scripture quotations marked (MSG) are taken from The Message. Copyright © 1993, 1994, 1995, 1996, 2000, 2001, 2002. Used by permission of NavPress Publishing Group.

Scripture quotations marked (NCV) are taken from the New Century Version®. Copyright © 2005 by Thomas Nelson. Used by permission. All rights reserved.

Library of Congress Cataloging-in-Publication Data
Names: Rose, Sarah Ann, author.
Title: Fearlessly Unshackled: Breaking free from the voice of destruction into your purpose and promise / Sarah Ann Rose
Description: Augusta: Integrity Publishing 2023. | Includes bibliographical references. | Summary: "Author Sarah Ann Rose shares with tremendous transparency how God unshackled her from a 30 year prison of anorexia."—Provided by publisher. Identifiers: ISBN 978-1-953822-03-1 (paperback) | ISBN 978-1-953822-04-8 (ebook)
Subjects: LCSH: Christian life.

Cover Design by Sara McGee
Interior Format by Holly Murray
Editing by Holly Murray and Sara McGee
Photography by Jae Ann Photography @jae_ann_photography

Printed in the United States of America

23 24 25 26 27   10 9 8 7 6 5 4 3 2 1

Dedication

Above all, I give glory to my Lord and Savior, Jesus Christ. In writing this book, I got to know Him even better and deepen my relationship with Him. God is a kind, loving Father whose desire is to bless me, and I am forever thankful.

A special thank you to my husband, who had many chances to walk away but stayed by my side. There were times I tried pushing him away, yet he remained loyal to me and our marriage. I love you.

To my beloved children—as I battle this affliction daily, I find solace and hope in you. You are the beautiful people God brought into my life, and I love you.

To my family—I'm sorry for any anguish I caused over the years. I love you and hold you all very close to my heart. Thank you for your love and support in my life.

Finally, I dedicate this book to those who wake up each day shackled by the voice of an eating disorder and to those helping someone with an eating disorder. May you find light and hope in this book. I pray you learn all things are possible with God and that it's okay to get help.

In writing Fearlessly Unshackled, I expose the inward struggles people try to hide. From the outside, it may look like we have it all together, but inside we are screaming for help. God is full of love and compassion. My prayer is that those who may not understand eating disorders will have the insight to extend His love and compassion to those in the struggle. Always be kind. You may never know the hope it extends.

Contents

Preface

As I consider sharing my story, I feel pinpricks of fear. This book exposes a secret part of my life. Many witnessed what I hoped they'd see, but never the depths of agony and torture that kept me shackled for years.

I struggled with body image issues from an early age and was diagnosed with anorexia in high school. I tried to keep it hidden, but drastic weight loss made me the topic of conversation in nearly every circle. Nothing I did on my own helped, and I even had some failed recovery attempts with recommended professionals.

The disease was debilitating and followed me into college, marriage, and as I began a family of my own. The eating disorder had a voice that started in a compelling nature to convince me to make changes in my routine, but ended up being a voice of complete control over my life. It affected every area. I felt unworthy, powerless, and humiliated. Even now, a heavy cloud of shame tries to press down on me, determined to keep me from revealing all I have kept hidden for years.

I desire to share my experience and what brought healing to my life in this book. Eating disorders like anorexia can be conquered. You can be unshackled from their grip. I press through the eating disorder's attempts to silence me now to bring freedom and hope to others.

I invite you to help me expose the lies of the enemy by reading and sharing my story, and step into a new season of freedom, purpose, and promise for yourself.

FEARLESSLY
UNSHACKLED

Author's Note

If you are reading this because someone you love is suffering with an eating disorder, thank you for taking the time to read and understand the inner workings of a life shackled by anorexia. I am sure it is frustrating and there are days you feel like giving up. Some days it may seem there is no light at the end of the tunnel and no way of escape. Fear traps us into thinking nothing will ever change. It steals hope and joy—both for the one overcoming the disease and the loved ones who are witnessing the struggles.

I always wondered why women who are in abusive relationships don't leave. My thought was, "Just get in your car and go far away." Yet I was the one who couldn't break free from the abusive relationship of anorexia for 30 years. It's easier said than done—but it can be done!

I pray your loved one will overcome the disease, but I know they will need you, your prayers, and Jesus. Love them, despite the frustrations you feel about how illogical it seems to you. And never lose hope.

The help of skilled professionals also played a role in my success. Knowing there was someone with experience who truly understood the science of eating disorders and knew what I was going through helped. They had the training to get to the root of the problem, walk me through it, and give me the tools to use in my fight while holding me accountable and cheering my victories. They didn't judge me—they empowered me.

3

Be willing to try different approaches until you find what works. Keep in mind that not only is this disease hard for the person going through it, but it is also hard for their loved ones. Counseling may be helpful for people on both sides.

I'm thankful I now have authority through Jesus over anorexia. Experience has taught me that walking in freedom from the shackles of an eating disorder is possible. I pray God touches your heart through the words of my story and that you see His hand reaching out to you. Grab hold of Him and don't let go. Know you are safe, loved, and cherished by the One who wants you to be victorious in every area of life.

Endorsements

Sarah's message of perseverance, faith, and hope will inspire you. Sarah's own formidable demon is anorexia. She speaks directly to fellow sufferers and those who love them, but her words will resonate much further. Anyone who has doubted their own value will recognize her battle, and find hope in her testimony.

We can all benefit from the call to be kind and act with love toward those around us. Sarah's vulnerability in sharing her story powerfully demonstrates that sometimes the people struggling the most are also the most adept at hiding their suffering.

-Debra Rodeghiero Johnston, MD

Sarah bravely shares insights from her 30-year journey with anorexia to encourage those who are courageously navigating their own battles, and to bring awareness and understanding to those who have a loved one fighting for their life. She provides a window into choosing life and pushing against the powerful voice of eating disorders and helps readers focus on seeking truth and God's love over and over again. You will find encouragement and hope within these pages.

-Megan Miller, LMFT
Restoration Ranch Retreat facilitator and consultant
Author, Lighthouse Collections: Beacons of Light in Life's Storms

This is a book that speaks honestly about living broken but beautiful. It's about all the amazing and terrible things that happen to us in our messy lives, and about the grace of God in the midst of it all. It is a book whose author states, "We are all beautiful, and God loves each one of us just the way we are." And because she shares her secrets, stories, and illustrations out of her own truth, we can all relate to a time when we, too, needed to hear these words of reassurance. Fearlessly Unshackled is a book that is blessed and promises to be a blessing to all who read it.

-Rev. Laura L. A. Overbo
Pastor, Lutheran Church of Our Redeemer

This book brought back memories of how difficult it is to see someone you love struggle with an eating disorder. If you are trying to figure out how to support an individual battling anorexia or a similar disease, this book will help. It is easy to see the physical devastation of an illness. It is hard to understand the mental anguish and know how to be supportive. This book delivers hope with practical solutions to those looking for the answer to the question, "will things ever change and get better?"

-Todd R.

Introduction

The alarm sounds. It's 5:45 and my stomach and arms are still burning from the day before.

"Let's go, Fatty Patty! Hurry! Get up! Let's go, let's go, let's go!"

The voice screams in my head as I jump out of bed, get dressed, and head to the equipment in the basement. I engage in a 50-minute workout followed by strength training five days a week, no rest for holidays. This is reduced from the twice daily, seven-days-a-week, 1.5-hour workout routine of previous years. I'm doing better.

If I miss a day, I hear the voice, "You think you're going to skip it? You're getting soft! Shame on you! Get up and get going, you lazy girl!"

When I finish, the voice continues, "OK, your workout is done; let's go, let's go, there are things to do! Did you pray? Did you mean it? Have you prayed for everyone? If you don't, something bad might happen."

The voice no one else can hear pushes and drives me through the day. Time for chores; ensure everyone has everything they need. I feed the first pen of horses. I love to watch them run up, and think, "There's my baby, Cutter, such a sweet boy."

"What?" the voice challenges, "if you love this horse, would you be feeding it outside? Someone who loves horses would bring them in and brush them morning and night. How can you say you love your horses and take good care of them?"

I want to scream back, "Shut up!" I can't. Instead, I go about the rest of my chores, replaying the words of failure and insignificance in my head.

Time to shower and get ready for the day. I hate showering and despise looking in the mirror. I hate putting clothes on in case they don't fit the way they should. Picking out my outfit, I get dressed, but the voice speaks, "Those jeans are a little snug on you, aren't they? Can't you feel that? They look snug across your hips and stomach, and look at those thunder thighs!"

My mind races. Maybe my jeans really are snug! Are they too tight? What did I eat yesterday? What did I do? Perhaps it's my workout routine that is making me have thick thighs!"

I rush to the mirror, and as I see the worried person looking back at me, I think, "I see it now! These jeans *are* snug and look horrible on me! I must fix this! OK, so my plan is to not eat today and do an extra workout later."

Everything goes quiet.

Then I remember I need to stick to my plan. I want to get better. I can't listen to the voice of the eating disorder.

Back and forth my mind tosses all day long in a battle of voices. It's real, and it's exhausting. I need to find a way to bring peace to the storm raging between my ears and freedom to my weary soul.

CHAPTER 1

Broken Dreams

Take delight in the Lord,
and He will give you the desires of your heart.
Commit your way to the Lord;
trust in Him and He will do this:
He will make your righteous reward shine like the dawn,
your vindication like the noonday sun.
Psalms 37:4-6

I look at the world and see others living, laughing, and having fun. But as I scroll through the social media façade, I realize how much hurt I've endured in my life. When did I become friends with the voice that relentlessly torments, terrorizes, and tortures my every moment? How long have I endured the misery? Where did the pain begin?

Being diagnosed with dyslexia made school hard. I was the kid getting special help. I was not a stellar athlete, so I did not form bonds of friendship by being on a sports team. My peers and I seemed to have no commonalities. I tried to blend in and go unnoticed.

Lunchtime was the worst. This is how it played out: get your food, scan the line to see if you knew anyone, and hopefully find someone kind to sit with for your meal. You didn't want to be an active participant, but you wanted to take up enough space so you don't appear alone.

I would have done anything to make a friend, then one day, I did. A girl in my class would write notes and give them to me after class, and at the bottom, she even wrote BFF! She would talk to me, and we would hang out. Best Friends Forever!

Fair-Weather Friends

There were some days, however, I would not get a note after class, and she would not talk to me. Worried I'd done something wrong, I would send her a note and ask her why she was not my BFF. She'd write back that I had not smiled at her, was not at her locker that morning, or that I had not walked with her to class. This pettiness continued throughout middle school and into high school. Finally, I had enough and never spoke to her again.

Any friends we'd shared kept following her and doing what she wanted them to do. Although I was relieved to no longer be living in constant anxiety wondering if I was doing what she thought I should do, I was alone again.

The Perfect People Pleaser

That relationship wasn't the first time I'd been under pressure to do what others thought was right. I remember walking into our elementary school's church service one day, yawning. The nun said, "Do not yawn in the house of God." I thought I was a bad person for yawning!

I was so ashamed to tell my parents how poorly I behaved and how much I had sinned by yawning in church. I believed I had to be perfect to receive the love of God. To be a good Christian, I needed to please God, my parents, and everyone around me. Failing would make God not want me. I didn't realize then how wrong that was. God wanted me to come to Him as I was, failures and all.

Come near to God
and He will come near to you.
James 4:8

Accept one another, then,
just as Christ accepted you,
in order to bring praise to God.
Romans 15:7

Sometimes, despite our best effort, things don't turn out as we dreamed. This doesn't make us a failure, it makes us human. We are flawed and imperfect individuals who have genuine emotions and failings, and regardless of our best attempts it is not possible to please everyone all the time. This is reality.

The Gift

There was once a small girl who dreamed of being acknowledged and valued by her parents. She longed for their love and acceptance, and strived to do everything she could to please them.

As part of her art class at school, the students prepared handmade gifts for Mother's Day. Committed to making something special for her mom to earn her love, the daughter worked hard constructing and painting every detail of a ceramic vase. She wanted it to be perfect.

After completing the project, she worked with the teacher to wrap it in newspaper and secure it in a box. She was so excited to get home and give her mom the gift. As she and her siblings were rushing to the bus, her toe

Things don't always
turn out like we

dreamed.

This doesn't make us a

failure.

It makes us

human.

caught the edge of the pavement. The box flew out of her hands and the vase shattered on the ground.

The little girl frantically began gathering the fragments, but the bus was about to depart. Disappointed, she left her mother's broken gift on the ground and climbed the bus steps before it pulled away.

On the way home, she watched her siblings as they held tightly to the presents they had made. She was so disappointed because she wanted to make her mother proud, and felt she had failed once again. When the bus stopped, their mother was waiting for them under the shade of the big tree in the front yard.

Her mother observed her daughter's empty hands, shook her head, and returned to the house with the other children. The little girl's heart was broken, and she ran to the tree, threw her arms around the trunk, and sobbed.

This is how I envisioned my relationship with God. The only thing I could bring him was me. My hands were empty. Like the broken vase, I thought I was too damaged to be put back together. I believed I was unwanted and displeasing to God.

It Can Be Different

But what if the story was different? What if, when the children stepped off the bus, her mother-saw her little girl's pain, fear, and broken heart? What if, instead of walking away, the mother ran to her daughter, picked her up, and held her tightly? She might tenderly whisper how much she loved her and how proud she was of her. She would ask the little girl to share all that was in her heart. Her mother would listen until she was done, and then remind her daughter how much she loved her and that she was there any time she needed her.

What if she taught this little girl about the merciful love of Jesus and how nothing she could ever do would be so wrong that Jesus would ever stop loving her? The little girl's eyes would have glistened in the realization of how much her heavenly Father loved and cherished her. A little encouragement and being taught how much Jesus loves her would have changed her whole story.

The Process of Imperfections

There is a story in Jeremiah 18 where God tells Jeremiah to go to the potter's house so he could receive a word from God. Jeremiah obeyed and watched the potter working with the clay on the wheel. Verse four says, "But the vessel that he was making from clay was spoiled by the potter's hand; so he made it over, reworking it and making it into another pot that seemed good to him" (AMP).

God was showing Jeremiah that He can rework us into a finished product designed to do something different than what we originally intended to do ourselves. There was an imperfection in the clay that the potter needed to work out. Only then could he shape the clay into the beautiful vessel. We need to allow God to mold and shape us so we fulfill His ultimate plan, and remember this is a process.

As imperfect and limited as we are, God's love for us is perfect and unlimited. He wants us to let Him work out our imperfections and mold us into something with a great purpose. He understands this is a process, and

God's love for us is

perfect.

and

unlimited.

along the way, He longs to hear our thoughts, heal our pain, and tend our wounds.

Psalms 147:3 says, "He heals the brokenhearted and binds up their wounds." Just as the little girl needed the comfort and instruction of her mother, God is always present to comfort and teach us when we feel broken. Wherever you find yourself, whatever dreams and expectations you've had, you have a Father waiting to bring the love, restoration, and healing for which you have been longing. He wants to take the imperfect, broken pieces of our life and recreate them into something beautiful with a divine purpose beyond what we might even imagine.

CHAPTER 2

The Fight

He gives power to the faint,
and to him who has no might He increases strength.
Isaiah 40:29, ESV

My name is Sarah. I am taking authority over anorexia, in Jesus's name. If you're living with an eating disorder, supporting someone with an eating disorder, or simply looking to learn more, I understand and I want to help. Gaining some insight about anorexia from my personal experiences and things I've studied is a good starting point for having the tools needed to gain some traction.

The statistics on the effects of eating disorders on young girls is staggering. It's no wonder my life was so affected when you consider eating disorders affect children at such an early age. Knowing that almost half of the girls in a first-grade classroom may already suffer from body image issues that can lead to this disease is a shocking realization. My heart yearns to reach out to all who deal with self-doubt and tell them they are beautiful; that God designed their body perfectly.

The National Association of Anorexia Nervosa and Associated Disorders (n.d.) gives the following facts from an extensive list:

Nearly 30 million Americans will have an eating disorder in their lifetime. Eating disorders are among the deadliest mental illnesses, second only to opioid overdose. There are 10,200 deaths each year as a direct result of an eating disorder—that's one death every 52 minutes. Statistically speaking:

- 42% of 1st-3rd grade girls want to be thinner.

- 81% of 10-year-old children are afraid of being fat.
- 46% of 9-11-year-olds are "sometimes" or "very often" on diets.
- 35-57% of adolescent girls engage in crash dieting, fasting, self-induced vomiting, diet pills, or laxatives.
- In a college campus survey, 91% of the women admitted to controlling their weight through dieting.

Thirty million people is roughly the population of Texas. With 9.2 million women in college in the US, 90% of them would be over 8 million women—almost the entire population of the state of Virginia (National Center for Education Statistics, 2022). Astounding.

I rarely say anything about someone's weight. You never know what they are hearing about themselves already. Being a society which looks to the media or anyone around us to validate our worth is unproductive. God created a special plan for you and you alone; no one else in the universe is just like you. You are an unparalleled creation, beyond comparison, designed for grand purpose!

See yourself through His eyes. Isaiah 43:4 tells us we are precious and honored in His sight and that He loves us. Jeremiah 29:11 confirms that He has good plans for us, that it is not in His plans to bring us harm. Oh, to grasp the depth of His love and breadth of His unique purposes for us. We would never fall prey to comparison and self-denigration if we only knew the extent to which the Creator of the world values us.

You are an

unparalleled

creation,

beyond

comparison,

designed

for great

purpose.

Anorexia Defined

The Mayo Clinic (2018) describes anorexia in the following way:

an eating disorder characterized by an abnormally low body weight, an intense fear of gaining weight, and a distorted perception of weight. People with anorexia place a high value on controlling their weight and shape, using extreme efforts that tend to significantly interfere with their lives. Anorexia isn't really about food. It's an extremely unhealthy and sometimes life-threatening way to cope with emotional problems.

It goes on to explain the difficulty in noticing the symptoms of anorexia because people conceal how thin they are, their eating habits, and any other physical problems they are experiencing (2018).

Over the last 30 years, my body was not always reflective of the reality of the struggle I was enduring. Someone may have seen me as a person of average weight, but they did not see behind the door. I may have looked fine on the outside, but I was restricting or able to maintain by only eating certain foods.

There was a time when I would only eat popcorn. In college, I would only eat pretzels. When my body appeared very thin, I would wear multiple layers of clothing under very baggy clothes.

It is not always possible to judge the severity of someone's pain and struggles just by observing them. I hid the reality, afraid to tell anyone or let anyone find out. Anorexia had created a distorted world for me as I believed the lies I heard within me.

Hiding the Signs

After struggling as long as I have, I learned to quickly see signs of it in others. It isn't because of what they look like on the outside, but certain behaviors that wave a red flag for me. I lived them, so I know them all too well.

I would not eat when others were eating. Sometimes I would say that I had already eaten or was too busy—that I would eat later. There were also foods I would avoid, stating it was for health reasons that I couldn't consume them—like being lactose intolerant or avoiding sugar because of false claims of hypoglycemia. Presenting a confident explanation would cause people to stop asking questions about what I wouldn't eat.

Talking about foods I enjoyed was easy, but going out to eat was difficult. I would order the same thing and eat at the same places. If I was offered something different, I would become very uncomfortable and decline. It was as if a voice in my head dictated my every move and it felt impossible to find something to eat the voice approved of.

Scales

I had a relationship with each scale I used, and I weighed myself multiple times a day. I knew which ones gave me a higher reading and which ones gave me lower readings. When I measured myself, I would check it to the quarter pound and preferred the scales with the cast-iron lever system like you might find in a physician's office. Their precision kept me from guessing my weight.

The reading of the scale was a miserable obsession which determined happiness. If the reading was high, it was a bad day. If it was down, it was a better day. No matter what, the voice never relented in my head; I always needed to weigh less.

Treatment

I am not a licensed recovery expert, but I can share my 30-year story of fighting and testify to the ongoing grace of God to help battle this disease. The Mayo Clinic explains that some of the biggest barriers to overcoming eating disorders is believing treatment isn't needed, being afraid of gaining weight, or thinking of the disorder as a lifestyle choice instead of an illness (2018). Further, while recovery is possible, it is important to monitor situations or stressors that trigger the onset or relapse of the disease.

It has only been within the last few years that I understood recovery is for me. And since God loves all His children and wants to see us all walking in victory, I can confidently say recovery is for everyone.

"Every person working towards recovery
starts in a different place, takes a different path, and
navigates the twists and turns that take them there.
Recovery is the process and is part of the journey."
(ANAD, n.d.)

I believe that recovery is possible, at any age and at any stage. While my words in this book do not replace professional support, I hope that sharing my personal experience can help someone find the same grace to overcome. God's Word says, "No temptation has

Recovery is for *everyone.*

overtaken you except what is common to mankind. And God is faithful; He will not let you be tempted beyond what you can bear. But when you are tempted, He will also provide a way out so that you can endure it" (1 Corinthians 10:13).

There is great hope in knowing God promises to provide a way out of whatever trouble we face. Sometimes we need to look for the way out or have someone help point us in the right direction, but escape is possible.

CHAPTER 3

How Do I Measure Up?

Praise be to the God and Father of our Lord Jesus Christ,
the Father of compassion and the God of all comfort,
who comforts us in all our troubles,
so that we can comfort those in any trouble
with the comfort we ourselves receive from God.
2 Corinthians 1:3-4

I recall one moment in high school when I was sitting around with others in my class and the boys were comparing me to another girl. One boy said I was probably five pounds heavier. Before then, I had never thought about my weight compared to someone else's, let alone considered other people were thinking about my weight.

My stomach dropped, and my face burned. When I heard them talking, I wanted to vanish—for the floor to open and swallow me whole as every eye turned my way. Were they all seeing this too? Did they all think I was fatter than the other girl?

My mind started turning. The other girl had lots of friends, and the boys liked her. Would more people want to be my friend if I could lose five pounds? I became aware and ashamed of my body and thought I needed to change it. My goal was obvious: lose weight no matter what. I never wanted to feel the sting of humiliation like that again.

Quest for Learning

Replaying the words "you are fatter than another girl" motivated me. I researched and learned about healthy eating. I read every magazine I could find. According to my research, milk was bad for you. Meat was a terrible choice, too. Eating butter and other fats makes people overweight. All the misconceptions and misinformation on food choice was dangerous.

Armed with my version of wisdom, I began. At first, it wasn't too hard, and I started slowly. I restricted a few things here and there and extended workouts to burn more calories. There was a thrill in seeing the results of working out and eating less. I weighed myself multiple times a day and could see the pounds falling off, and it was rewarding.

And I realized I was never alone. I had a new companion in the form of a voice in my head directing me what was right and wrong—what I should and shouldn't eat or do. It began to dictate my every move.

The Voice

When I was hungry, the voice would step in. "If you are hungry, that is good. That means you need food, and if you do not eat food when you need it, your body will take all the fat away." The voice would remind me of the day when I'd first learned I didn't measure up and how I'd felt.

I reinforced the voice by comparing my size to others. I would find pictures of myself and look for areas where I could see fat. I compared clothing sizes to my body measurements. If my body was not the smallest size, the voice in my head would repeatedly taunt, "You are fat, you pig. You are not working hard enough."

The more I listened to the voice, the more powerful it became and the more control it had over my life. The words escalated as it gained more control. "You are not just fat; you are dumb and ugly. No one likes you. You are

The voice we listen to

most

is the voice with the

most control.

disgusting; who would want to be friends with you? Who would want to date you?"

The Science

The voice I was hearing is a known phenomenon. Registered Dietitian Shena Jaramilla (n.d.) describes the voice this way: "The ED voice (eating disorder voice) is the toxic inner dialogue we have with ourselves regarding food choices, weight, or body image when we experience an eating disorder." According to Matthew Pugh (2020), "The EDV/S (eating disorder voice or self) is usually seen to enter individuals' lives during periods of insecurity and instability. For others, critical internal voices are present before the onset of disordered eating but intensify alongside the emergence of ED symptoms."

Chris Thornton (n.d.), a clinical psychologist and the clinical director of The Redleaf Practice, referred to a study by Pugh and Waller (2016) which he said showed that as eating normalizes, "the power of the eating disorder voice will decrease." He further stated, "Those who have undergone the process of nutritional restoration and weight regain will often report that the voice gets worse as it is challenged by healthy eating behavior and recovery." But he added, "However, after a period of weight being stable at a healthy weight and normal eating, the voice diminishes over time."

My Reality

It was hard to go without eating, at first. I would feel hungry and irritable. But the more I did it, the easier it got. The more I listened to the voice, the more I pushed people away from me. I was not meeting up with friends or spending time with family. The voice became my only friend.

Real-world problems didn't hurt as much because I focused on what I could control. I controlled what I ate and how much I exercised. If something bad happened, someone was mean to me, or someone hurt me, I would hurt myself more by not eating or by over-exercising.

The only truth I trusted was on the scale. When the number on the scale was going down, things were good. When the number rose, I would spin into hysteria. To handle the anxiety, I engaged in negative self-talk. I would say, "maybe if you hadn't eaten that slice of bread or if you had worked out longer, this would not have happened." Then the voice had an open door to continue to shun and reprimand me.

The voice always seemed innocent in the beginning. "You are fat. I will help you get skinny. We need a weight loss plan. We need an exercise plan."

As I became desensitized to repeated criticisms, it became more aggressive, attempting to get my attention and make me obey. The voice was critical of my appearance, spoke that I didn't fit in my clothes, and drew attention to anything unflattering to cause me discomfort or shame. Then the voice intensified further, turning hostile. "You are a worthless human being. You let everyone down. Can't you do anything right? You are an embarrassment." I chose not to eat because the pain of being hungry was better than the pain of hearing the voice; yet the voice was determined to break me down.

CHAPTER 4

Slowly Taking Control

> But Jesus said to them, "My Father never stops working,
> and so I keep working, too."
> John 5:17, NCV

The stronghold of anorexia was a gradual process. The more control the eating disorder's voice had, the stronger anorexia became. As the eating disorder grew, I would lose more weight. I lost a lot of weight. The more weight I lost, the more people noticed, and their comments only propelled the voice in my head.

The voice reminded me it was not enough and twisted their words. It said, "they are tricking you. They are lying, Sarah. You must have been huge for them to say you look good now that you've lost weight."

As my weight continued to drop, I looked sick—like I had a terminal disease. The outline of my bones was quite distinct. When I brushed my hair, it came out in clumps. I had peach fuzz all over my body. I was oblivious to everything but the fat. People would make comments about what they saw, so I started wearing baggy clothes. I concealed my body so no one would ask me questions.

The Lies

Anorexia turned me into an expert liar. I hated lying, and I hated myself for lying, but the voice dictated my decisions. It ensnared me in a web of deceit. I felt trapped, caught between the fear of opposing the voice and the guilt and shame of lying to those who loved me.

People would ask me if I'd eaten, and the voice would feed me a lie to respond. "I already ate, I'm not hungry." or "I'm not feeling well." It's like my mouth would open, and the lie on my tongue spilled out as if it were butter on a hot roll.

Rather than go to lunch, I would go to the library to study so people at school didn't notice I wasn't eating. It was important to pay attention to the school menu, however, so I could reply to the question of what I "had" for lunch. Accuracy was important or they would discover the lie and realize I'd not eaten.

I would buy food and throw it away. This provided evidence to support the lie of, "see here's the receipt, I ate it in the car." I would take food to my room rather than eating with the family. Studying was the excuse, but the food ended up in the trash, flushed down the toilet, or hidden in my room.

Soon, I would only listen to the voice of the eating disorder. I isolated myself. The voice shackled me to the lies, and I couldn't break free. What started with controlling food now controlled every part of my life, and nothing I did was good enough.

Guilt and Shame

There came a point when people were so worried they tried to force me to eat using guilt and fear. They said: "What are people going to think of you being this skinny?" "How can you put people through this?" "This makes your grandmother so sad." Then there was the oh-so-simple-fix, "Just eat." I felt like I had ruined my life and the life of everyone around me.

Trying to guilt or shame someone dealing with an eating disorder does not solve the problem.

Guilt and shame may make a person feel pressured to eat, and they may comply, but it's challenging when they've been eating nearly nothing for months or even years. I remember consuming only a set number of items I had calculated. Once I even attempted to calculate the calories in a single aspirin.

When pressured, I would take a bite of a sandwich. My brain would tell me, "Don't they know there's starch, protein, and some type of condiment on that sandwich? There's no way I am going to do this."

It would become a tipping point for me. I'd yell and say I hoped they never talked to me again.

Some people would go away because they thought I was crazy, and my circle of friends would get even smaller. Others stuck it out a little longer and tried to help.

Well-Meaning Intentions

People suggested I talk to someone local for "professional help." This local "professional" person did not even know about eating disorders. Treating someone with an eating disorder is complex. It can take months for someone inexperienced to diagnose an eating disorder if the person dealing with it keeps it well concealed, and I was not ready to talk.

It all came to a head my junior year of high school. I was skin and bones. My mom had tried everything she knew to do. I had her believing the cat was making me sick. She told the doctors, and I can only imagine what they thought.

It was difficult for her to face the fact that I had an eating disorder—a mental illness. Now that I'm a mother, I can guess how much it hurt her to see me struggle. My children mean more to me than my own life, yet my mother had to witness her child dying, one skipped meal at a time.

Internal Conflict

Everyone loves a fairy tale ending. I wish I could say I graduated from high school, attended college, married a fantastic man, had a wonderful family and a beautiful career, and was no longer a prisoner to the shackles of anorexia. But the road to freedom was not so simple.

Recovery is hard. The internal conflict between what I knew I should do for my wellbeing and the voice of the eating disorder never ceased. Working alongside my dietitian, conversing with a counselor, and having a doctor as part of my support system enabled me to be in better shape as I completed my senior year.

I did graduate high school and college. I married a great guy and am blessed with an incredible family. I even have a career I'm passionate about. While it sounds like a fairy tale, it has not been easy to unlock the lies of unworthiness and shame that held me bound for so long.

> Before they call I will answer;
> while they are still speaking I will hear.
> Isaiah 65:24

Progress

Through the process of gaining my health, I realized I was also in a spiritual battle. There was a voice working to keep me from achieving God's promises in my life. While the voice in my head speaks to me about food, it also weakens the faith I have in myself, my trust in God, destroys my happiness, and harms my relationships with family and friends. It attempts to keep me a prisoner and in despair. This voice belongs to our enemy—the devil.

I've learned there is a difference between the fear of God and fearing God. God is powerful and, in awe, I consider all He has done for me. He is so good. He is pleased with who He created me to be and has never been waiting for the opportunity to punish or shame me if I didn't hold to His standard. He was ready with an answer and heard me when I called out for help (Isaiah 65:24).

I learned God wants to shine His light on me and through me to lead others to know Him better. God is the rock from which I stand in my fight to conquer anorexia.

The Truth

The recognition of the power of God, His love for me, and that the voice was my enemy wasn't a transition that happened overnight. Unlike the romantic drama films of today where the heroine has a revelation, the sun rises, and cheerful music plays while birds chirp in the background, my understanding was a longer journey. A cloud lifted, and I saw things differently. It felt like I was slowly waking up and seeing slight differences in and around me. It had me wondering if God had always had these blessings in my path, but it was only now that I could see them. These blessings were the keys to unlocking my prison. While the voice I'd heard for years was real, I discovered I now had the power to defeat it.

There was a voice

demanding

my attention,

and another

beckoning

me to true freedom.

CHAPTER 5

Something Smells Fishy

But I tell you the truth, it is to your advantage that I go away;
for if I do not go away, the Helper (Comforter, Advocate,
Intercessor-Counselor, Strengthener, Standby)
will not come to you; but if I go, I will send Him
(the Holy Spirit) to you [to be in close fellowship with you].
John 16:7, AMP

The path of recovery is not an easy one. People in recovery might slip back into bad habits. They may feel it is easier to stay with what is "safe" and familiar, or even want to quit. I have been there and some days I am still there. I've used the excuse of, "I am too busy to eat or make food."

Like most people, I am running back and forth between work, meetings, and kids' events. I also don't enjoy cooking. The kitchen is the last place I want to be. I would rather be outside or be doing something productive.

I often get comfortable with "safe" foods. I deem something "safe" if it is something I can eat without giving it much thought or preparation. Tuna salad was that for me in my 40s. I would eat spinach leaves with a can of tuna, cheese, and dressing. At first, I only ate it for supper, one or two nights a week. Then it became every night, then it extended to lunch, too.

I did that every day for two years! Seven days a week, 365 days a year, tuna was my go-to for lunch and supper. I bought tuna in bulk and rationalized my decision. Tuna was good for you, cheese was a superb source of calcium, and leafy greens had many health benefits. There were other effects, too. First, our house smelled like tuna all the time, and I went through quite a few can openers.

People would ask me, "Do you ever get sick of tuna?" I did, but I decided it was "safe." I didn't have to battle with the voice telling me it would make me fat, and I believed the ingredients to be healthy choices as well. Then, one day, I started having severe headaches and not feeling well.

The Math on Poison

A random thought popped into my head, "What is mercury poisoning?" I decided to do some research and found there was, in fact, such a thing called mercury poisoning and I realized I had the symptoms. Further research showed that the FDA recommended a maximum of 12 ounces of tuna per week.

I did the math. Tuna came in 6-ounce cans. I was eating 12 ounces twice a day, seven days a week. That calculated to the recommended amount being 4,380 ounces of tuna per year and I was eating 61,320 ounces of tuna per year!

I then researched, "what happens when people eat too much tuna?" I found it could lead to mercury poisoning, and according to my research, it caused a multitude of health issues from pain in the extremities, tooth loss, memory impairment, trouble sleeping, and even death. Even with the possibility of death on the table, my immediate thought was that I wanted to keep my teeth!

Researching mercury poisoning had been a divine intervention from God. I decided I needed a check-up. I was too embarrassed to go to my regular family doctor, so I went to another clinic and did a walk-in visit. When I met the doctor, I was not about to tell her I had consumed over 120,000 ounces of tuna in the last two

God is still

in the business of

divine

interventions.

years. Instead, I told her I ate tuna a lot. The bloodwork revealed high levels of mercury in my blood. She then instructed me not to eat any fish for a year!

As someone battling an eating disorder, I faced quite a dilemma. Tuna was safe, easy, and I could do it every day (so I thought). Now, I had to find something new. I went through periods where I ate only baked potatoes, steamed cauliflower and cheese, sub sandwiches, or bagel sandwiches with cheese and tomato. The pattern of eating only one type of food for a season kept my mind from having to answer the question, "What should I eat today?" There was a season when I would only eat a certain number of baby carrots, counting them repeatedly to ensure I did not eat too many.

It is easy to fall into life patterns. Some patterns, like reading God's Word every day, are always good, no matter how much of it you do. With some patterns, however, you need to fight back and tell the voice of the enemy he will not run your life!

When the Spirit of Truth comes,
He will guide you into all the truth,
for He will not speak on His own authority,
but whatever He hears He will speak,
and He will declare to you the things that are to come.
John 16:13, ESV

Jesus tells us in 1 John 4:1, "Beloved, do not believe every spirit, but test the spirits to see whether they are from God, for many false prophets have gone out into the world" (ESV).

When I hear a voice in my head commanding my decisions, I need to test it and see if this voice is from God. The eating disorder voice, I can say with confidence, was not the voice of God.

God has a better way for us, and He who is in us is more powerful than our enemy in the world (1 John 4:4). I am thankful Jesus sent the Holy Spirit to walk closely with us. He is the helper we need. The prompting of the Holy Spirit led me to research more about the effects of tuna. It was a case of "too much of a good thing" not being good at all!

The God of peace will soon crush Satan under your feet.
The grace of our Lord Jesus be with you.
Romans 16:20

When I listen to the voice of the eating disorder and do not take care of my body, it is a temptation of the enemy. When I feel I cannot fight the voice, I think of the scriptures that tell me I can. God wants to give me peace and take away the torment. I visualize Him getting mad, stomping on Satan, and demolishing the enemy's voice, which comes to me through the lies of anorexia. That's when I stomp my foot, declare the voice of the enemy to silence, and adjust my thoughts.

Luke 10:19 says, "I have given you authority to trample on snakes and scorpions and to overcome all the power of the enemy; nothing will harm you." This verse promises me I can trample the enemy. I see myself as the warrior. Satan may shoot arrows of lies at me, but I can hold up the shield of faith God has given me. The shield quenches every fiery dart the enemy sends (Ephesians

6:16). Let that warrior emerge from within you. Fight the enemy with the sword of God's Word, knowing that His shield of protection deflects the enemy's ammunition.

CHAPTER 6

I Can See You, but I Can't Hear You

But those who hope in the Lord will renew their strength.
They will soar on wings like eagles;
they will run and not grow weary,
they will walk and not be faint.
Isaiah 40:31

As the cloud of the eating disorder slowly lifted from my mind, I realized how little I could see and hear. A haze surrounded and insulated me from the words of those who cared.

I remember when my mother sat at the foot of my bed weeping, telling me her fear of my dying. I had no words to offer, and my gaze was emotionless. My belief was that if I ate, I would die, or death would come from the torment of anorexia. The voice controlled every thought and action. I saw her tears; I saw her pain, yet I was immobile.

Years later, my husband watched me struggle with this disease. He tried to be the voice of reason, providing practical advice. As an engineer, he uses logic in his decision making. If a + b = c, then it must be true.

An eating disorder, however, is not logical. The voice would steal every positive conversation, twisting and turning my husband's words in my head. His logical responses would speak the truth, and my responses would rebut him.

"I like that shirt on you," he would say.

"I think it makes me look fat," I would respond.

"No, it doesn't make you look fat. I don't know what you're talking about!"

"So, my other shirts make me look fat, but this one doesn't?"

"No! No shirts make you look fat. I don't understand how you can see it that way, Sarah."

"Well, that's because you're not seeing it right."

Back and forth, the conversation continued until he no longer knew what to say.

Because my husband and I have been through a few seasons with this eating disorder, he notices when it raises its ugly head. When he sees me eating the same thing repeatedly, not eating at all, or exercising obsessively, that's a cue he picks up on. When he sees me pushing myself away from friends and relationships, he pays attention. These are all signs that the eating disorder's voice is getting louder in my head. The louder it gets, the deeper into myself I can crawl.

He may comment that it looks like I'm going backwards, and I'll respond, "I'm not going backward. I'm doing what I need to do." He'll give examples of what he has seen, as I defend the behaviors as if my life depended on it.

It's then that he asks, "Sarah, when was the last time you talked to your counselor? Have you been in to see your doctor recently? I'm worried about you."

Hearing his genuine concern about the reality of it all is always a wake-up call for me now. It makes me mad when I think I'm going around the same mountain again. Why did I let anorexia take over? I was doing so well, and it snuck back in, taking hold little by little.

Help

If I'm in a place where I can admit I have a problem, I reach out to my counselor. She can read me like a book. We have built such a trusting relationship over the years that I can speak honestly about what's happening. We work together as I climb back out of the hole again.

I know what it feels like to have that overpowering voice running through my head. I know what it feels like to be defensive about my behaviors when everyone around me can see the demonic influence trying to sneak in to take control again.

This cycle often brings feelings of shame. I've worked so hard, so how did I let myself slip?

I've learned not to focus on those negative thoughts, but on what I can do to move forward. My key is in recognizing that I slipped; my triumph is seeking help.

I desire to honor God in my life through all I do. That is why I am forever grateful Jesus knows we are going to slip up sometimes. He's always reaching out with His ever-loving arms to pull us out of these trenches, forgive us, and help us rise above the darkness so we can soar in victory.

God is waiting

to pull us out of the

trenches

and into His

arms.

CHAPTER 7

Compromised Plans

Many are the plans in a person's heart,
but it is the Lord's purpose that prevails.
Proverbs 19:21

I have come to know the tactics of anorexia all too well. The feeling of being out of control or not knowing what will happen next overwhelms me. It makes me feel like I cannot breathe or focus. But as long as I have a plan in place, I can push through.

Failed Plans

I had a perfect nourishment plan for the week. I knew exactly what I would do and what meals I would eat each day, but an unplanned opportunity came to meet friends for dinner. I'd already eaten breakfast and lunch when they invited me, and there was no escaping the invitation without being awkward. I could hardly call and say, "Hey, this is Sarah. I have anorexia, so if you could explain your menu for tonight, the ingredients you put in your main course, and how you plan to cook it, that would be great!" I could not cut things out from the meals I'd already consumed, and I had no control over what my friends would be serving.

My mind raced with questions: Are they going to cook with butter? Will they fry or grill the food? Will they serve red meat? What if they have mashed potatoes? If they make vegetables, will they smother them in butter and cheese?

As my thoughts spun out of control, I knew I needed a new plan. I considered how I could go but get out of eating. Perhaps I could explain I'd already eaten, but could join them for a drink. What if I said I had a stomach bug? If I have a stomach bug, could I still go to their house?

The reasoning continued. I couldn't get out of eating, but I could try to take a bite of a few things and move the food around on my plate to make it look like I ate. I huffed, knowing that wouldn't work. Pushing food around would start an interrogation about why I didn't like the food, and I didn't want to be rude. Worse still, what if they thought I didn't like the food and offered to make something else? They'd assume I didn't like their cooking, or I was some type of vegan, vegetarian, or a granola-eating hippy. I didn't want to be humiliated.

I considered eating enough to be polite. Then the mental negotiations with the eating disorder began. "If I eat supper tonight, then I will not eat breakfast or lunch tomorrow. That will be safe." My mind slowed down, and I felt comfortable with the plan.

Then, a thought came to mind, "Oh wait! What if they serve dessert? I have eaten nothing sweet for over 20 years! I can't do that!"

Yes, it's true. I'd had no birthday cake, no licking ice cream in the heat of the summer, and no sips of hot chocolate to remove the chill on a cold winter day.

"So what should we do about dessert?" the voice asks. "What believable illness could you have that would prevent eating desserts?"

"Hypoglycemia?" I would think back. "My dad has that. Maybe I could say I have hypoglycemia. Can people with hypoglycemia have even a little taste? Ugh! That will not work!"

The whole scenario of an evening ending with dessert unfolded in my mind. There would be a big production as they place some wonderful monstrosity on the table. Everyone would be excited as the oohs and aahs spilled from lips, watering in anticipation.

I can hardly refuse dessert. I can't say I'm on a diet— look at me! I'm thin—they would never believe that. Maybe I could politely take some. But if I even tasted it, how will I compensate for the sugar and calories? I've planned to miss breakfast and lunch tomorrow to cover for supper tonight. Finally, the answer comes—I'll wake up an hour early and exercise for two hours instead of one.

It's these kind of tricks the eating disorder plays on my mind. The negotiations lead to a compromise. But what am I compromising? I'm once again shackled, a prisoner to anorexia. The voice of the enemy entraps me to steal my happiness, joy, and freedom. A simple dinner invitation feels next to impossible for me.

Freedom Granted

I'm working to recognize the truth that God wants me free. Free from the shackles, free from this bondage. The voice of the enemy wants me to compromise and is bent on deceiving me. I have the power to say no, and to ignore that voice. God created this amazing earth with an abundance of nourishment. He wants us to take part and enjoy the variety He created for us. He wants us to enjoy godly friendships, laughter, and the feelings that come with a healthy community.

The enemy wants to isolate us and occupy our mind. He wants to take every magnificent gift God intends as a blessing and keep us from it. He will use any method of deceit he can.

The enemy desires to steal

every magnificent

gift of God

and to isolate us

to keep us from

experiencing

God's

blessings.

When I think of opportunities I've missed, when I allowed this influence to dictate my life, it frustrates me. The enemy has tormented my best intentions and made it difficult to walk in the fullness of God. John 10:10 says, "The thief comes only to steal and kill and destroy; I (Jesus) have come that they (His people) may have life, and have it to the full."

What a blessed promise that is! I don't need to restrict the foods I eat the next day or exercise to compensate for enjoying something good God designed for me. God has a purpose and plan that exceeds even my own well-thought-out plans! God wants me to have a fully abundant life; I will not allow the enemy to take that from me. He will not take my peace, my community, my family, or my marriage from me. He will not keep me shackled.

A compromise comes about when both parties in a dispute give up something they want—each side making concessions until both sides agree. When I argue with the voice and make compromises, the only one who really loses is me! We don't need to compromise the promises of God. He provided them all for us, and they are ours! Ecclesiastes 3 says there is a time for everything— weeping, laughing, mourning, and dancing. I have done plenty of weeping and mourning. It's time to laugh and dance!

CHAPTER 8

Isolation

> Only be careful, and watch yourselves closely
> so that you do not forget the things your eyes have seen
> or let them fade from your heart as long as you live.
> Teach them to your children
> and to their children after them.
> Deuteronomy 4:9

Imagine not being able to see and experience the world around you. What if you'd been dreaming of something substantial and, at the last moment, someone snatched the dream away? That's precisely what the eating disorder did. It held me captive, took experiences away, and ended relationships.

Growing up, I'd always dreamed of going to see Garth Brooks. I wore out cassette tapes of his music! Well, the opportunity to attend a concert came, and my husband and I had tickets. My dream was about to come true!

The day of the concert, the voice got strong. "It will soon be time to go. Your husband is planning on dinner before the show or afterwards. How are you going to hide not eating? You can't fake it. He's going to know."

I found myself bound by anorexia again. I wanted to go to the concert, but I could not leave home without the voice trying to take over. I was going to face going to a restaurant with my husband if I went to the concert, and that felt like more than I could handle. Since the voice told me I did not have a way to avoid eating, it also told me I was going to miss yet another opportunity.

Because of this persistent internal battle, I told my husband that I did not want to go to the concert. I missed a once-in-a-lifetime opportunity to see Garth in concert, all because of the press of the enemy, and I could not reason my way out of bondage.

Missed Opportunities

I am sad to say that the list of things I missed is extensive. I did not want to wear a bathing suit, so I would not get in the water to play with my children. If I ever did, I spent the time thinking about my body instead of enjoying their smiles and laughter.

There were only a few restaurants which served food I would eat, so I controlled where we ate. I would cook dinner for my family, then go do other things while they ate. I would not attend "take a parent to lunch day" with my children because I could not eat what they served. Invitations to lunch or dinner with friends were most often declined. If I needed to travel, I brought my food. I was so consumed with the voice that I could not fully experience the joys God had laid out before me.

There were times when I would do anything to follow the voice of the eating disorder. While the lies started small, they began creating a life of their own. It would convince me I wanted to be by myself, that people didn't really like me, or they only invited me over to make fun of me. It made me think people talked behind my back and laughed as soon as I looked away. Not only did it control thoughts regarding food and exercise, it held me captive using fear of what others thought or might do to isolate me. The voice controlled every part of my life.

Knowing every gathering included food made the thought of attending festive celebrations exhausting and miserable. I made excuse after excuse for missing family functions or declining invitations from friends. They didn't understand because I didn't let them in my life enough to see the truth of the battle I fought. Eventually, people stopped asking. I really needed their help and encouragement in those tough moments. The most heartbreaking thought is those people needed me in their life, too, and if I'd been honest about my personal struggles, we may have been able to fight the battle together.

Therefore encourage one another
and build one another up, just as in fact you are doing.
1 Thessalonians 5:11

God's Plan

How amazing that God created this beautiful world for us to experience! He wants us to live life with unspeakable joy. He wants to bless us and wants us to see and delight in all He has made. The glory of God surrounds us and He is calling each of us to live our life to the fullest potential—to fulfill every plan He designed for us when He made us.

For we are God's handiwork,
created in Christ Jesus to do good works,
which God prepared in advance for us to do.
Ephesians 2:10

Moses

Could you imagine the result of Moses responding, "No, not now," at the burning bush when God called him to lead the Israelites out of Egyptian captivity? What if he'd said, "I have a few other things to do right now. Can you put out this fire and give me a raincheck?"

Moses didn't put God on hold, however. Exodus 3:4 reads, "When the Lord saw that he had gone over to look, God called to him from within the bush, 'Moses! Moses!' And Moses said, 'Here I am.'"

Now granted, after he found out what God wanted him to do, he felt great fear about his personal limitations and wanted God to send someone else to do the task God had in store for him. But, God knew the strengths and weaknesses of Moses. He wasn't concerned about his limitations, He just wanted Moses's yes! Moses obeyed God's call. God told Moses He would be with him and teach him what to say and do. He even provided a helper for Moses in his brother, Aaron. God used Moses mightily and his yes to God's call freed an entire nation.

Samuel

What about the child Samuel, who, while he was sleeping, heard God's call and woke to do His bidding? What if he'd responded, "Sorry God. I am too sleepy to listen to Your voice." Instead, he responded, "Speak, for Your servant is listening" (1 Samuel 3:10b).

The story of Samuel reminds us that we are never too young to hear and obey God's voice. Samuel was willing to be inconvenienced, to listen to and obey God's call. Even though it made Samuel uncomfortable, he shared the message God gave him to share, and it came to pass exactly as God said. The Word says, "The Lord was with Samuel as he grew up, and He let none of Samuel's words fall to the ground" (1 Samuel 3:19). Can you imagine if God backed up everything you said and made it happen?

Your

yes

brings

freedom

to others.

Caleb and Joshua

The Bible also tells the story of Caleb and Joshua, two of twelve spies Moses sent into Canaan to scout the territory that was God's promised land to the Israelite nation. When the spies returned to report all they'd seen, they all agreed on the richness of the land. Ten of them, however, added that the current inhabitants were too powerful to be defeated and their cities were as impenetrable as fortresses.

Caleb and Joshua dared to contradict the report. Numbers 13:30 says, "Then Caleb silenced the people before Moses and said, 'We should go up and take possession of the land, for we can certainly do it.'" But the Israelites chose to believe the negative report. They couldn't see themselves victorious, even with God on their side! What a surprising conclusion to draw, given the miracles they'd already seen leading up to their escape from the tyrannical rule of the Egyptians!

God was angry with their lack of faith and declared that not one person who'd witnessed the signs He performed in Egypt and the wilderness and still disobeyed His command would ever see the land He'd intended to bless them with when they began their journey out of Egypt (Numbers 14:20-23). They wandered in the desert until the entire generation had died—all except Joshua and Caleb. When the Israelites returned 40 years later and set about conquering the land, the same giants which had terrified the original spies proved no match for God and His people. The circumstances of the enemies facing them hadn't changed, only their faith and trust in God had changed! God came through as He had promised!

Lessons Learned

We are God's children, and we want to be faithful to go where He leads us. When we are obeying His commands, there is no need for fear. Joshua 1:9 says, "Have I not commanded you? Be strong and courageous. Do not be afraid; do not be discouraged, for the Lord your God will be with you wherever you go."

Even if we feel as unqualified as Moses did at the burning bush, like Samuel, we can hear God's voice and bring miraculous freedom to others. Even when something looks impossible to overcome, we can trust God to conquer any plan of our enemy without fear, like the children of Israel.

The Bible tells us God has given us gifts, and He expects us to be faithful stewards of those gifts (1 Peter 4:10). If He has given us gifts with the expectation of our using them, He wouldn't plan to set us up for failure. God will supply all we need for anything to which He is calling us. He also gave us the gift of the Holy Spirit within us to be our helper!

Who is on the other side of your yes? To what is God calling you? What is the best thing that could happen if you agreed to go after all He has for you? How exciting that God has gifts for us, and even more thrilling yet is they have purpose beyond just for our personal blessing.

God always has people on His mind. And knowing we might bring an argument of inability to the table, He provided the Holy Spirit to be our helper. We also have a world full of brothers and sisters in Christ who also have been blessed with gifts. When we partner in unity, what an even greater impact we make on those around us. You never have to do life alone.

To one there is given through the Spirit
a message of wisdom,
to another a message of knowledge
by means of the same Spirit,
to another faith by the same Spirit,
to another gifts of healing by that one Spirit,
to another miraculous powers, to another prophecy,
to another distinguishing between spirits,
to another speaking in different kinds of tongues,
and to still another the interpretation of tongues.
All these are the work of one and the same Spirit,
and He distributes them to each one, just as He determines.
1 Corinthians 12:8-11

I wish I had considered these stories of faith when I had Garth Brooks tickets or the chance for lunch with friends and family or swimming with my kids. I missed so many opportunities that would have been a blessing to me and other people. Hindsight is like that. Looking back, we see mistakes we've made and doors we could have opened or left closed.

While I can't change my past, I can remember the lessons I've learned and make different choices today! Deuteronomy 4:9 encourages us not to let lessons go to waste, but to teach future generations from our experiences. So today, I choose to forgo isolation and, like Moses, change generations to come by stepping out in faith and doing things I may not feel qualified to do! I choose to obey God's call and walk in freedom for myself and others.

CHAPTER 9

Triggered

Be kind and compassionate to one another,
forgiving each other, just as in Christ God forgave you.
Ephesians 4:32

'm not a sports kind of girl. If you throw a ball at me, it will most likely hit me square in the face. I might think to duck or throw my arms to block it. The natural reaction for some would be to grab it. Those are the people you want on your team. They have the right instinct for the game.

Trigger

A trigger causes a reaction. Throwing a ball could be a trigger. For those who are sports-inclined, they might get excited and catch it. For me, my reaction hopefully would be to duck to avoid a bruised cheek.

Mention weight, well, that's a trigger, too. So is comparing the way I look to someone else or when I hear others talking about how much weight they gained over the holidays. When I'm unprepared, the enemy has used these triggers to cause me to spiral into an unhealthy place.

I've had people look at the food on my plate and comment, "Wow! That's a lot of food! Aren't you worried it'll make you fat?" Hearing those kinds of comments makes me want to snap! They are often triggers for people dealing with an eating disorder.

In high school, my counselor challenged me to eat a cookie at Christmas. My grandmother had beautiful cookies on her table that year. People would stop by the table, take some cookies, and comment on their amazing flavor. Trying to determine which one I would pick, I hung around the table, eyeing my choices. I was excited to conquer my counselor's challenge! I finally made my choice and reached for the perfect cookie.

One of my family members said, "Be careful! Those cookies will make you fat!" This person knew I was struggling, but didn't realize the degree to which the comment would hurt. The spoken words kept me from successfully completing the challenge.

The voice of the enemy often chirps in, reminding me to analyze everything day by day, meal by meal. I replay it all in my mind. If I am not busy planning, I am often replaying my food intake.

This same voice sometimes even convinces me I have eaten things I haven't just because of the conversations I have heard from others around me. I cannot always separate what is true from what is not.

I think that is why it is so hard for people to understand eating disorders. When looking at someone dealing with anorexia, you may see a very thin, sickly person. That person, however, looks at themselves in the mirror and sees fat. It's not truth, but that is their focus.

It's important to consider what may be a trigger for others. While we can't walk around on eggshells all day, every day, worrying about saying the wrong thing, we can opt to be mindful of the needs of others. Ephesians 4:32 challenges us to be kind and compassionate. You don't know what someone is battling right now or how they may receive the things you say or do. Even the expressions on your face can be misinterpreted or interpreted negatively. We never want to cause an unhealthy trigger, and the easiest way to prevent that is to remember people around us are all facing struggles that we know nothing about. When we walk in constant awareness of God's love for us and try to model that love for others, we are less likely to say or do anything unkind.

Our Thought Life

Our thoughts are powerful, and we would be wise to remember we are waging war against the enemy and his tricks. He knows that the more he can keep us thinking about and believing the lies he is telling, the less time we will have to do the good works of God.

When lies from the enemy rush through your head, you have the power through Jesus Christ to put a stop to it. We can follow Jesus's example when a thought becomes a hindrance or an obstacle. Matthew 16 tells the story of Jesus sharing with His disciples about God's plan to save mankind by allowing Jesus to die and be raised back to life. Upon hearing this news, Peter immediately responded with a resounding *no*!

While Peter didn't want to see Jesus die, his statement was in contradiction to what Jesus knew was the only way to make Heaven a reality for us. Jesus knew God's perfect will. He looked past what was comfortable for Himself, past His own will, and saw our need for salvation. Jesus rebuked Peter quickly. He didn't want to give the thought even a moment to become an idea on which to meditate. There was no other way for mankind to be saved, and Jesus kept His will in line with His Father's will by shutting down the voice which disagreed with it.

Matthew 16:23 tells us, "Jesus turned and said to Peter, 'Get behind Me, Satan! You are a stumbling block to me; you do not have in mind the concerns of God, but merely human concerns.'" Peter was one of Jesus's

When

lies

from the enemy

rush through your head

you have the

power

to stop it.

closest friends, yet Jesus brought correction when needed and put a stop to what Peter was saying.

When a thought that does not line up with God's Word and His character comes to our mind, we must not dwell on it, but quickly put an end to its power by saying and meditating truths from God's Word instead. Remember these lying thoughts don't come from God, and they keep us from living in the freedom and joy He wants for us.

> Do not conform to the pattern of this world,
> but be transformed by the renewing of your mind.
> Then you will be able to test and approve
> what God's will is—His good, pleasing, and perfect will.
> Romans 12:2

The Word tells us to renew our minds. The Greek definition of renewing our mind is to adjust "our moral and spiritual vision and thinking to the mind of God, which is designed to have a transforming effect upon the life" (G342, n.d.). We can know God's mind because we have His Word! We are to adjust the way we think and how we see things to how God thinks and how He sees things. In doing so, we are changed. It is then that we can discern His plan for our life.

The Word also commands us to "take every thought captive to obey Christ" (2 Corinthians 10:5b, CSB). The enemy will whisper lies to your mind, but the more you can crush them under your feet, the stronger you will be. When it is hard, call on the Holy Spirit to help you fight. Ask His presence to be with you; to help you shift your mind to focus on the good things of God.

The

Holy Spirit

is ready

to help you

fight.

Finally, brothers and sisters, whatever is true,
whatever is noble, whatever is right,
whatever is pure, whatever is lovely,
whatever is admirable-if anything is excellent
or praiseworthy-think about such things.
Philippians 4:8

Your mind is powerful. Use the Word of God to come against the lies. The Word is truth! We will not accept the lies of the enemy. We can fight and overcome them, and we have the most powerful person in our corner—God.

CHAPTER 10

Now I See

Consider how the wild flowers grow.
They do not labor or spin.
Yet I tell you, not even Solomon in all his splendor
was dressed like one of these.
Luke 12:27

There are many ways God communicates. He speaks of His ability to provide while I watch the birds on a cold winter day. He provides food and shelter for them, and His Word tells us He loves us more than the birds (Luke 12:7). His voice speaks as I watch the rain fall on the grass after a hot, dry day. His voice is in the wonder of watching a newborn colt stand up just minutes after coming into the world. It amazes me how God provides everything we need.

Take puppies, for example. They play, jump, yip, and roll around, oblivious to anything but the joy of the moment. If God provides such a carefree existence for a puppy, wouldn't He do the same for you and me? The world is miraculous. God provided every need for everything He created. He has done the same for us. He wants us full of joy, and He is willing and able to help us if we trust Him.

Hebrews 6:18 says, "These two things cannot change: God cannot lie when He makes a promise, and He cannot lie when He makes an oath. These things encourage us who come to God for safety. They give us strength to hold on to the hope we have been given" (NCV).

Yes, my soul, find rest in God; my hope comes from Him.
Truly He is my rock and my salvation;
He is my fortress, I will not be shaken.
Psalms 62:5-6

Hope comes from God. He gave us promises in His Word, declaring we are more than conquerors, and nothing is impossible for Him. I can hold on to those promises because I know He can't lie. With the truths in His Word as my tool, I am breaking the chains with which the enemy shackled me!

No matter the situation you face, start with the Truth. While I know the voice of the eating disorder will lie to me, God never will. I can always go to God for safety and truth.

I know God loves me. The Bible says in 1 John 4:9-10, "This is how God showed His love among us: He sent His one and only Son into the world that we might live through Him. This is love: not that we loved God, but that He loved us and sent His Son as an atoning sacrifice for our sins."

It can be difficult to even begin to fathom the love God has for us, because inside, we sometimes struggle with loving ourselves or we project our human understanding of love on how we interpret God's love.

I look at myself and sometimes feel unworthy of love. I see everything I have done wrong or the people I've hurt. If anyone could see inside my heart or mind or know the things I am ashamed of, how could they love me? God knows these things, yet in 1 John 4:8, we see the words, "God is love." And because love is His identity and His Word tells us of His great love for us, we know He

God's
Word

provides the tools

to break the

chains.

will love us no matter how obnoxious, mean, hurtful, vengeful, hateful, prideful, or undeserving we are. Knowing the things we would say and do, He still loved us first. And no matter how many times I miss the mark, He will still love me. I want to be worthy of that kind of love, yet I could never earn it. But there's no need to try to earn His love, anyway. Like salvation, His love is a gift I only need to receive.

> For it is by grace you have been saved, through faith—
> and this is not from yourselves, it is the gift of God—
> not by works, so that no one can boast.
> Ephesians 2:8-9

Sometimes I feel like I am wearing a T-shirt that reads, "she has been obnoxious, mean, and sometimes hurtful." It can feel like everyone sees it, and that they can see all the faults I try to hide. It makes me want to wrap myself in a cloak of shame and hide away from God and everyone else.

When we think this way, it can become a prime breeding ground for the enemy to mess with our heart and mind. He latches on to this shame and tells us lies about ourselves, our unworthiness, or that God won't forgive us this time—we don't deserve it, so don't even bother asking. But no matter how many times we circle the same mountain, we never circle the drain with God. His Word promises in 1 John 1:9, "If we confess our sins, He is faithful and just and will forgive us our sins and purify us from all unrighteousness."

No matter how many times we circle the same mountain,
we never circle the drain with God.

God knows every thought I've ever had or will have, and I may sometimes worry He will see something He doesn't like. But when He looks at His children, even though He knows when we have made wrong choices, had impure thoughts or motives, or even blatantly done things contrary to His Word (again!), His love for us never fades or fails.

Shame

I have used food as a weapon to hurt myself. Anorexia has pulled me into unhealthy patterns. There have been times I've felt shame and regret. I've lied, been hateful, obnoxious, mean, and sometimes hurtful. But I want to be better.

Do you hold on to shame from the past? Is there a hidden box in your heart that you sometimes pull out and reopen? If so, *stop*!! Jesus overcame shame. He promises to forgive our sins so we can live in peace.

God cannot lie. God tells us He loves us. He knows all, sees all, and *still loves* us. He has made a way for us to live life to the fullest.

Consider the parable of the lost sheep found in Matthew 18:12-14 and Luke 15:3-7. Jesus tells a story about a shepherd with 100 sheep. One of them wanders off and gets lost. The shepherd searches for the lost sheep until He finds it, then celebrates its return.

God knew we would sometimes get lost and do things we regret. He doesn't want us to run away and hide in our shame. In fact, He pursues us! He wants us to come to

Him, talk to Him, and ask Him for forgiveness. When we do, He will forgive us, free us from shame and guilt, and He celebrates that we have come to Him.

Getting caught up and listening to the enemy's voice is easy. He wants us captive to his lies. Lying is the enemy's primary weapon against God's children. He uses the tactic of deceit to separate us from our heavenly Father. This is not the will of God.

We can break the shackles of lies and shame the enemy uses to make us feel bound and separated from God. The enemy's goal is to prevent us from living the life God has promised us. God has big plans for us, but if we keep believing the enemy's lies, we cannot fulfill God's will.

So consider the lilies. Think of all the ways God takes care of everything in His creation. Cast all your cares on Him (1 Peter 5:7) for He cares for you! Don't let shame or regret hold you back any longer. Ask Him for forgiveness, receive it and the fullness of His love! Matthew 6:26 tells us to look at the birds and think about how God cares for them. It goes on to say, "Are you not much more valuable than they?"

No matter how many times

we circle the same

mountain,

with God,

we never circle the

drain.

CHAPTER 11

What About Fearing God?

"His pleasure is not in the strength of the horse,
nor His delight in the legs of the warrior;
the Lord delights in those who fear Him,
who put their hope in His unfailing love."
Psalms 147:10-11

Growing up in the Christian faith, I have read and heard about fearing God. Hidden away in my mind was the idea that I should fear God—He was large, intimidating, merciless, and awaited my making a mistake. In my mind, He was a giant, walking around the earth watching me and making note of all my sins.

Imagination

I imagined one day I'd walk up to the pearly gates of Heaven, behind which someone stood, clipboard in hand. He would hold out a ream of paper—the notes of my life written in red ink. There would be pages and pages of things I'd done wrong and, seeing the list, I couldn't dispute it. Next, a door would open, exposing a wall of utter darkness, and as I took the first step, I would drop into the fiery inferno of hell.

When I was young, this is what I thought God was like. I would look at photographs of Jesus and all the children surrounding Him or piled onto His lap as He told them a story—but I never saw myself as one of those kids. In my imagination, I was always the kid standing at the back in whom Jesus had no interest. Jesus knew my transgressions. Why would He want me?

Psalm 147:10-11 reinforced that vision in my mind. But one day, when I was in my thirties, I listened to someone sharing about God. They were talking about His immense love for everyone—including me! I thought this concept strange; didn't they realize that if they didn't behave properly God wouldn't love them? Yet these people were so confident in God's love for them they appeared content with their life and future, and had a joy that I just didn't understand.

When they messed up, they admitted it. They asked God to forgive them, which liberated them from their sins. I thought, "They must be living in Whoville!" I'd never been taught about God this way. I watched and listened to them, thinking, "wait until Judgement Day." I felt sure they would be in for a surprise. There was no way God was as good as they said.

Judgement

I don't know who I thought would be good enough in God's eyes to make it past the pearly gates. My grandparents were old and nice; they would probably make it through. Not me, though. Never me.

Some believed God was fond of them, and they could communicate with Him, asking for help. I saw in black and white the command right there in the Bible—fear God. I considered the people who thought God loved and listened to them to be quite lucky.

Several years later, I talked to a friend to help me process my thoughts. She explained that fearing God meant having high esteem for Him, a reverent admiration of His holiness, and amazement at His incredible works. I considered her words and decided I had that!

> Let all the earth fear the Lord;
> let all the people of the world revere Him.
> Psalms 33:8

I studied further and came across some words from Mark Altrogge. He wrote:

God commands us to fear Him and says that He takes pleasure in us when we fear Him. Why? Does He enjoy us being afraid of Him? I know I don't want my children to be afraid of me. I want them to love me and enjoy being with me.

To "fear Him" means to stand in awe of Him.

To fear the Lord is to stand in awe of His majesty, power, wisdom, justice and mercy, especially in Christ—in His life, death and resurrection—that is to have an exalted view of God. To see God in all His glory and then respond to Him appropriately. To humble ourselves before Him. To adore Him.

We tend to be in awe of worldly power, talent, intelligence, and beauty. But these things don't impress God because "His delight is not in the strength of the horse (mighty armies, worldly power) nor His pleasure in the legs of a man (human strength)."

But God delights in those who fear Him—those who stand in awe of Him—and instead of trusting in their own human abilities or resources, "hope in His steadfast love." (2017)

We should be amazed at God's goodness, power, and love, and grateful for all the great things He has accomplished. He wants to lend a hand to us, to help us in our daily struggles, to be a sounding board and to even speak back to us in His Word and in so many other ways.

How long had I tried to fight anorexia on my own? I did not need to depend on my strength to fight, but on His. How amazing that He has the strength to help us— in the big and small ways!

Rushing Things

Have you ever watched someone struggle to do something, and you want to rush in and do it for them?

I wanted to teach my 80-year-old grandfather how to use email to stay in touch with my family and me. He lived many hours away, and the only way for him to email us was using a keyboard plugged into a hole in the back of his television. He would need to select the right input using his remote control, then use the keyboard to navigate the screen to get to his email.

My husband and I set it up for him and we were visiting for several days to teach him. He was so excited about learning. We walked him through the steps, then let him try. It was a struggle.

Sometimes we would just all start laughing because he would get so mixed up on the steps. It wasn't until we wrote step-by-step instructions in large print that he could work the new technology on his own. We all need guides in our life to help us find our way.

In today's world of instantaneous satisfaction, we expect things right away. You can purchase a pair of shoes using an app on the phone and get an immediate thank you email with a tracking number soon to follow. I can view the location of my shoes from the moment they're shipped until they deliver the package to my front door! Talk about instant gratification!

Speaking to God is even faster! God is always listening, and you're important to Him. He can hear your thoughts and knows the desires of your heart even before you do. He speaks back—but are we listening? His voice becomes more obvious as I obey what I'm hearing and trust Him in that process. I ask God for direction and let Him guide me. When I sense His peace, I know I'm following His plan and trust He will make a way.

In Psalms 147, the author, David, spends the entire chapter talking about the goodness of God. We never have to hunker down in fear of God striking us for every wrongdoing. He isn't impressed with our abilities—He is the one who gave them to us! As we read the Psalm (listed below) we remember to celebrate how amazing God is; how much He loves and cares for us. It is a reminder of God's power and goodness, and a call to worship.

I wonder if there are times God sits back and gets a chuckle on my behalf, like my husband and I regarding my grandfather's lack of technological understanding. Often, I don't see and understand the goodness of God all around me. I can be impatient to have things go my way right away. He has given me His Word, but I sometimes try to do it all on my own.

God's help is a call away. It takes no set-up and there is no delay in Him hearing your prayers.

He is listening and willing to help us with open hands. Praise God! He truly is good.

Praise the Lord!
For it is good to sing praises to our [gracious and majestic]
God; praise is becoming and appropriate.
The Lord is building up Jerusalem;
He is gathering [together] the exiles of Israel.
He heals the brokenhearted and binds up their wounds
[healing their pain and comforting their sorrow].
He counts the number of the stars;
He calls them all by their names.
Great is our [majestic and mighty] Lord
and abundant in strength;
His understanding is inexhaustible [infinite, boundless].
The Lord lifts up the humble;
He casts the wicked down to the ground.
Sing to the Lord with thanksgiving;
sing praises to our God with the lyre,
who covers the heavens with clouds,
who provides rain for the earth,
who makes grass grow on the mountains.
He gives to the beast its food,
and to the young ravens that for which they cry.
He does not delight in the strength (military power)
of the horse,
nor does He take pleasure in the legs (strength) of a man.
The Lord favors those who fear and worship Him
[with awe-inspired reverence and obedience],
those who wait for His mercy and lovingkindness.
Praise the Lord, O Jerusalem! Praise your God, O Zion!
For He has strengthened the bars of your gates,
He has blessed your children within you.
He makes peace in your borders;
He satisfies you with the finest of the wheat.

Fearlessly Unshackled

He sends His command to the earth;
His word runs very swiftly.
He gives [to the earth] snow like [a blanket of] wool;
He scatters the frost like ashes.
He casts out His ice like fragments;
who can stand before His cold?
He sends out His word and melts the ice;
He causes His wind to blow and the waters to flow.
He declares His word to Jacob,
His statutes and His ordinances to Israel.
He has not dealt this way with any [other] nation;
They have not known [understood, appreciated,
heeded, or cherished] His ordinances.
Praise the Lord! (Hallelujah!)
Psalms 147:1-20, AMP

CHAPTER 12

Trapped

Fearlessly Unshackled

> I will walk about in freedom,
> for I have sought out Your precepts.
> Psalms 119:45

People who knew I struggled with an eating disorder often asked me if I wanted to get better. I did, but anorexia trapped me in a tangled web—the lies, pain, and fear surrounded me.

At fairs or outdoor events in the Midwest, they often have puppies for sale. Kept in a temporary, circular, gated area, the puppies can see out, and potential buyers can see in—great marketing! Who can resist a pen full of cute puppies?

The puppies watch the world from the confines of their pen. They may see another dog pass by and get excited. They watch children laughing and playing. Some puppies watch with wagging tails. Others jump at the fence in excitement as if saying, "Let me out! I want to play with those children! I want to chase that dog! I want to experience the world outside of this little pen!"

Sometimes I feel like this excited puppy. I look out from a controlled and restricted world. I see all these adventures people have and the relationships they're building. They are laughing, having fun, and enjoying life. Like the puppy, I want to shout, "Let me out! I want to experience life like that!"

Other puppies observe the world outside their pen, interested in what is going on, longing to be part of something, but appear timid regarding what that might mean. Both the excited puppy and the watchful puppy hope for something different.

The zoo is quite a contrast. When I visit the zoo, I love seeing all the animals, but something doesn't sit right with me. Many of the animals seem lethargic and uninterested. They may live their whole lives in these cages. Workers constructed each environment to represent their natural habitat, but it lacks the richness and dimension of the real world. These animals seem complacent. They have no hope for anything other than their present condition and may have never even known real freedom.

Sometimes, like the puppies, I look out at the world with hope. I feel excited and energized to fight anorexia. The trap is that while I may find myself ready to jump the gate to run and play, fear causes me to retreat.

Other times, I have felt more like a caged zoo animal—hopeless and trapped by the fabricated environment in my mind. Complacency envelops me as I realize the world I've built for myself, constructed by the lies of a dismal reality, will be all I may ever know. This, too, is a trap. It's a lie from the pit of hell whispered until I believe it.

It is Good

Instead, I need to break down the barriers of the self-manufactured environment in which I find myself. There is beauty all around us, and God wants us to be part of this glorious world and has a significant role for each of us.

He is always present and knows our needs. Some people have a God-given gift for helping those who struggle with eating disorders like anorexia. They have the knowledge and expertise to guide others along the journey of redemption so that we may experience the joy, excitement, and beautiful things around us that God created.

In Genesis 1:1-19, we learn about the creation of the world. The Word says in verses 1-5:

In the beginning, God created the heavens and the earth. Now the earth was formless and empty, darkness was over the surface of the deep, and the Spirit of God was hovering over the waters. And God said, "Let there be light," and there was light. God saw that the light was good, and He separated the light from the darkness. God called the light "day," and the darkness He called "night." And there was evening, and there was morning—the first day.

With each day of creation, there is one phrase repeated, "And God saw it was good." In fact, 1 Timothy 4:4a affirms, "For everything God created is good." Proverbs 16:4 says, "The Lord has made everything for its own purpose" (AMP). Looking at these verses, we know everything God created–from the very beginning–is good and has a purpose. How reassuring!

Genesis also tells the story of the first man and woman—Adam and Eve. Created for good, for communion with God Himself, they succumbed to the lies and temptations of Satan, and brought sin and shame upon the earth. In a world where everything was perfect, Eve still believed the lies of the enemy.

Father of Lies

The enemy is still lying to people. How often do we believe what the deceiver speaks? He still whispers in my ear, "That has too much fat; you cannot have it. There is sugar in that; do not eat it. If you eat, you need to do some physical activity to work it off. Remove anything that gets in your way of achieving your weight loss goal." He will tell me not to eat, skip meals, and eat only certain things.

He tries telling me not to worry about having friends. They dislike me anyway. He asks me when they even called me last and why is it I always have to be the one to call and check on them? Maybe this is because they don't want to be with me, I hear him suggest to my mind. So, I withdraw. I keep myself isolated to avoid being further hurt.

Even though I know the truth and even though I'm walking in recovery with God every day, the enemy never stops trying to get me to believe his lies. And he doesn't quit trying to find a weak moment when I'm feeling a little self-conscious or distracted.

When I believe and fall prey to the lies, I may have a momentary sense of control. I may even be able to justify my decision to agree with the lie. But the root is always a lie. Any perceived sense of control or happiness is only temporary.

The voice makes me feel incapable of doing things for myself or others. It tells me I am not smart enough, good enough, or talented enough. It tells me I'm not able to achieve the goals I've set for myself. The voice says I should not speak in front of groups because I'm not a talented public speaker. It whispers that disabilities and diagnoses make it impossible to write a book to tell my story. The voice tries to make me feel too afraid to try. I do not want to fail in my goals or calling, and the lies of the eating disorder try to steal self-confidence. He feeds

The

root

of any promise

from the

enemy

is always a

lie.

me lies to distort reality. If I believe them, I feel like I'm forever doomed, like there is no escape.

When I hear these things, I must remind myself again of the scripture in John 10:10. It is the thief who comes to steal, kill, and destroy. He wants to steal, kill, and destroy my peace, joy, freedom, confidence—my very life. He doesn't want me to walk in God's goodness and he doesn't want me to point anyone else in the right direction, either.

First One Tactic, Then Another

As soon as I recognize the lies and from where they come, the enemy tries a different tactic—shame. My cheeks may get hot and a heaviness may come over me as I consider the diseases of dyslexia, cancer, and anorexia which have been named at various points of my life on my medical chart. I may consider how they could keep me from succeeding in what God is calling me to do. What will people think of me? Who do I think I am? How can I achieve these dreams with my limitations?

It may even take me a few minutes to realize where my thoughts are spiraling. And when I don't take my thoughts captive, I become the one shackled. And he never quits trying to weigh down my soul with his schemes, lies, and manipulation.

In Luke 4, we learn about the temptation of Jesus. Even after Jesus defeats the enemy, verse 13 says, "That completed the testing. The Devil retreated temporarily, lying in wait for another opportunity" (MSG). When the first lies don't work, he uses anything else he can to get a foothold and regain control. And he never quits trying, so we can't quit fighting back.

Believing the Truth

God does not disapprove of my shortcomings. Instead, we read in 2 Corinthians 12:10, "for when I am weak [in human strength], then I am strong [truly able, truly powerful, truly drawing from God's strength]" (AMP). I can draw my strength from the one who not only created me and gave me life, but also who gave me the ultimate gift of His life!

God loves me and wants a relationship with me. That is the truth. The enemy will always lie. He will say that God will give up and His mercy will run out. But God does not give up on any of us. He did not send His Son to the earth to show us how to live, pay the ultimate price of dying for us on the cross to save us from sin, just to give up on us when we hit a bump in the road. Like the one lost sheep, He comes after us when we stray from the fold.

Jesus took all our sins and shame on His body to set us free from it all. His sacrifice enables us to have a relationship with God and live with Him forever in Heaven. God will not push us away because we make new mistakes. He invites us to recognize them, come to Him, and say, "Father, forgive me."

God never grows weary of listening to His children. In fact, Jesus told us to keep on asking, keep on seeking, and keep on knocking (Matthew 7:7, AMP). Jesus died on the cross so that we would have freedom from sin and freedom while we remain on this earth. We realize the expanse of our freedom through studying His Word. Galatians 5:1 says, "It was for this freedom that Christ set us free [completely liberating us]; therefore keep standing firm and do not be subject again to a yoke of slavery [which you once removed]" (AMP). The freedom Paul referred to in Galatians was the freedom that comes from being God's children. God made a beautiful world for us, His kids, and He wants us to experience the joy within it.

So I commend the enjoyment of life,
because there is nothing better for a person under the sun
than to eat and drink and be glad.
Then joy will accompany them in their toil
all the days of the life God has given them under the sun.
Ecclesiastes 8:15

CHAPTER 13

Afraid to Live

Therefore let us [with privilege]
approach the throne of grace
[that is, the throne of God's gracious favor]
with confidence and without fear,
so that we may receive mercy [for our failures]
and find [His amazing] grace to help in time of need
[an appropriate blessing, coming just at the right moment].
Hebrews 4:16, AMP

Recovery can be scary. After years of familiarity, I faced the challenge of leaving what I knew and embracing a new unknown. The voice of the eating disorder had left me feeling heartbroken, lacking self-assurance, and unable to trust anyone or anything. I'd been conditioned to listen to that voice instead of the voice of God.

I knew I couldn't keep anorexia and its voice a secret and needed to share with someone who could help, but I feared what people would think of me. I believed others would think I was a vain, shallow person who worried about being skinny. I thought they would judge me or expose some deep, dark secret I didn't even know existed.

How would they "fix me?" What if they did things I wasn't comfortable with them doing? I processed many worries, and the enemy did anything he could to keep his hold.

Finding Help

When I was a teenager, my parents were desperate to help me. I did not want to go to an in-treatment facility. I did not want to be away from my horses; they were the only things I was living for. My mom worked to find all the options available. We found and chose an outpatient option.

My mom would take off work and drive me to treatment. Money was tight, and treatment wasn't free. There were people who did not understand why I needed this level of help. Some said it was just rebellion and for my parents to force me to eat.

It was hard for my dad to understand, at first. He is a fixer by nature and wanted to fix me. But even though he did not understand the complexity of anorexia, my dad still supported me.

There were some tough patches. My parents bought special food for me. Often, I would not eat it or throw it away. During that season, it was tough to be around me. If I was not crying, I was mean and combative. There were times I behaved like the average 3-year-old, throwing things or flailing around on the floor kicking and screaming. I was trying to be hard to love so they would leave me alone.

The Emotional Battle

I felt like I embarrassed my parents back then. What would they tell their friends and our family? I cost them money and did not appreciate the help. In fact, I despised help and would do anything to get out of it. I did not comprehend the burden they carried. They wanted me to be happy and healthy. I wanted to get better but was also angry about needing help.

I felt guilty.

The waters of life will not always be smooth, but there is a way to make it through any situation we face. Isaiah 41:10 says, "So do not fear, for I am with you; do not be dismayed, for I am your God. I will strengthen you and help you; I will uphold you with My righteous right hand."

You are not alone; God will not abandon you. Jesus hears and sees all and carries us through whatever comes our way. Jeremiah 32:17 says, "Ah, Sovereign Lord, You have made the heavens and the earth by Your great power and outstretched arm. Nothing is too hard for You." Life can be hard for us, so it is comforting knowing Jesus is with us, not overwhelmed by our circumstances, and able to help. Nothing is too hard for Him!

Psalm 31:24 (KJV) says, "Be of good courage, and He shall strengthen your heart, all ye that hope in the Lord." When I close my eyes, I envision Jesus with His arms wrapped around me. The strength of Jesus radiates through me, and I can feel it. It brings me a feeling of security and comfort. Anorexia has no power over me when I keep my mind focused on Jesus. My strength comes from Him, and His is the voice to which I will listen.

Philippians 4:13 (KJV) says, "I can do all things through Christ which strengtheneth me." When I read this passage, I think of things I never thought were possible for me and how Christ showed up and gave me the strength to get through them. We can always go to God when we have a need. He has mercy available when we make mistakes and has enough grace to help us, no matter the size of the need we face!

Anorexia

has no power
when I keep my mind

focused

on

Jesus.

For I am the LORD your God
who takes hold of your right hand and says to you,
do not fear; I will help you.
Isaiah 41:13

No temptation has overtaken you
except what is common to mankind.
And God is faithful;
He will not let you be tempted beyond what you can bear.
But when you are tempted,
He will also provide a way out so you can endure it.
1 Corinthians 10:13.

Romans 16:20 reminds us that God is more powerful than the enemy. Remember that when Satan tries to convince you otherwise. They are not "equal opposites." There is, in fact, no comparison between God's power and the power the enemy tries to wield on earth. Satan only has the power we give him. God has all power and authority. Call on God to help you overcome the lies. According to Luke 10:19, God gave you the authority to trample on serpents and scorpions, and over all the power of the enemy. Nothing shall by any means hurt you! How powerful!

When fear comes knocking at the door, if you feel afraid to live, know that you aren't alone in the fight! Satan even tempted Jesus, but Scripture tells us in Luke 4 that Jesus never gave in to the temptations and defeated the enemy using Scripture as His weapon!

I have felt the desire to give in to the eating disorder. I could believe the lies or yield to the taunts and false promises. But Jesus exemplified the right way to respond to the enemy using the Word of God to correct half-truths and outright lies. He was persistent in His use of Scripture to defeat the enemy. I, too, need to shut down the voice of the enemy, and to do so consistently—each time the enemy comes to attack my peace.

When I think of the words "Man cannot live on bread alone," I am reminded of the temptation Jesus faced and how it was not about the food, but about knowing and following the Word of God. God created me and He lives in me. God desires for me to have a life full of joy, not be afraid to live! He adores me, and I am His unique creation.

I am aware of the enemy's attempts to deceive me, and I am striving to break the pattern of negative thoughts and behaviors to achieve the freedom that God desires for me. God's help is always available. I will no longer be afraid to live. I choose to pursue the abundant life God has planned for me.

I will not die but live,
and will proclaim what the Lord has done.
Psalms 118:17

CHAPTER 14

Overcoming Regret

For You, O Lord, are good,
and ready to forgive [our sins, sending them away,
completely letting them go forever and ever];
and abundant in lovingkindness
and overflowing in mercy to all those who call upon You.
Psalms 86:5, AMP

The enemy never stops looking for ways to trip us up, and replaying past mistakes to stir up feelings of guilt was a common tactic used against me. Satan didn't want me to live free and shine brightly. He wanted to keep me his prisoner, so I didn't bring freedom to others.

Crafting a plan with my counselor was an essential tool to fight anorexia's hold on me. It ensured I didn't exercise to the extreme and helped me have a plan for my meals that would be nourishing. We also worked on ideas to do new things that would challenge the voice of the eating disorder. I get comfortable with certain things, so when I add new types of food into my plan, it is a challenge. But the more challenges I overcome, the stronger I get and the freer a life I can live.

Some challenges were easier than others and I felt a sense of pride in conquering them. Some challenges were a little more difficult, and I didn't meet them with any level of success.

Regret often accompanies failure, which can make me feel things are spinning out of control. I learned that a quick word of positive reinforcement helped bring balance and slow the spin. Simple phrases, "Great job! I am so proud of you!" or "That was really hard, but you did it!!" went a long way in affirming each baby step I

Satan
wanted to keep me his

prisoner

so I didn't bring

freedom
to

others.

took. If it was on the plan, I would check it off and congratulate myself. If it was new and not on the plan but I ventured out, I added it to our list and put a big star by it. Experiencing daily successes was thrilling! I would then follow up with my counselor and share the success!

New Things

I tried to say yes to new experiences and opportunities. Gatherings of people often involve food and socialization. This can be hard for someone like me who is overcoming an eating disorder. My husband and I attended a basketball game, and a group of our friends suggested we go out afterwards. Instinctively I put up a wall, declining their offer. The voice in my head said, "you should go home and eat what you normally do. Do not venture out or try anything new."

Recognizing the voice in my head not being the voice of God, I knew that this would be an opportunity for me to challenge myself! I know most people would consider appetizers after a game to be of little consequence. For me, these fried and breaded foods were a hard thing to consider eating. But I accepted the challenge and met it with success!

But oh, boy, how the voice took over the following morning. The pressure was intense, and the voice in my head was loud. "How could have you done that? What are you going to do to cut back today?"

God's Plan

I knew I needed to dig deep and reach out to our Lord and Savior, Jesus Christ. I trusted He would give me strength and in Him, all things are possible. I wanted to have relationships with people, and I knew this was God's plan, too. He wants us to laugh and connect with others. Relationships give us an opportunity to share Jesus and to give them an opportunity to see His goodness in us. We cannot do that if we're sitting at home alone every night. We need to put ourselves out there and know it's okay to have fun in the life with which He has blessed us.

When the enemy comes against our freedom, remember we are not alone. We can push back and deny him the right to our life. As we recognize the lies and tricks of the enemy, remember how much stronger our Lord is. Jesus wants good and joyful things in our life! Opportunities will come that feel more like challenges, but we can fight back and kick the enemy to the curb!

> You make known to me the path of life;
> You will fill me with joy in Your presence,
> with eternal pleasures at Your right hand.
> Psalms 16:11

> "For I know the plans I have for you," declares the Lord,
> "plans to prosper you and not to harm you,
> plans to give you hope and a future."
> Jeremiah 29:11

God wants you to have a joy-filled life. He wants to use you. He created you and has amazing plans for your life. God will be with us and when we call on Him. He will strengthen us.

It may be easier to avoid trying something new, but I also know what a false sense of security develops when you limit who you are and what you can do. God has big plans. He wants to see you prosper in the good works to which He calls you.

Find Strength in Your Gifts

Imagine how Mary felt when the angel told her she would be pregnant. How afraid she must have been! She had not had relations with a man and was engaged. Her betrothed could have had her stoned because she was pregnant outside of marriage. But Mary found strength in her love and trust of God to fulfill the assignment He had for her.

Like Mary, God has placed special things inside of you. These are just for you. No one else in the world can use the gifts He has given you like you can. And, like Mary, you are called to share these gifts with others.

We can trust and follow our Lord. He will provide all we need, and even when we face difficult times, He is with us, prepared to help us come against the enemy and walk with us to victory. A life lived in obedience is a life lived without regrets. His desire is to pour blessings over us as we commune and walk with Him.

Overcoming Regret

The Lord is my shepherd, I lack nothing.
He makes me lie down in green pastures,
He leads me beside quiet waters, He refreshes my soul.
He guides me along the right paths for His name's sake.
Even though I walk through the darkest valley,
I will fear no evil, for You are with me;
Your rod and Your staff, they comfort me.
You prepare a table before me
in the presence of my enemies.
You anoint my head with oil; my cup overflows.
Surely Your goodness and love will follow me
all the days of my life,
and I will dwell in the house of the Lord forever.
Psalm 23:1-6

CHAPTER 15

Out of Control

Pray in the Spirit at all times.
Pray with all kinds of prayers,
and ask for everything you need.
To do this you must always be ready. Never give up.
Always pray for all of God's people.
Ephesians 6:18, ERV

I remember a time in my life when I felt threatened and unsafe. Things happened I did not want to have happen. I cannot recall the exact moments or details, but I remember being violated through persuasion as a child. I remember being warned that if my parents found out, they would be angry and would accuse me of wrongdoing. Whenever I tried to resist the perpetrators, they threatened and shamed me. There is a scripture in Matthew that triggers these vague memories. The passage tells the story of Satan tempting Jesus in the wilderness. The enemy says, "'All this I will give you,' he said, 'if you will bow down and worship me'" (Matthew 4:9).

Relinquishing control can be scary—if you're giving up control to someone who doesn't have your best interests in mind. In the verse from Matthew, Satan was trying to convince Jesus to give up His control and authority, but never had Jesus's well-being in mind. Satan was and always will be self-serving.

For years, I've tried to understand the root of fear regarding giving up control. I want to follow God with all my heart and mind, but submission to His authority brought conflicting emotions. I remember having to do exactly what someone in power forced me to do, and being threatened if I didn't obey.

When Jesus asks us to obey Him, however, it is from a place of love, not from a desire to dominate and control. His heart is like that of a parent watching out for their child, wanting to keep them safe, healthy, and happy. This is the heart of Father God. He wants us to follow Him and walk in obedience to His Word because this will lead to joy and peace in our lives. Giving the control to Him brings ultimate freedom, and He will never take advantage of that control. His heart for us is only good.

I praise you because I am fearfully and wonderfully made; your works are wonderful, I know that full well.
Psalms 139:14

Clean

I am uniquely and wonderfully made by God, our creator. He knows all and sees all. He knows my heart. It saddens Him that someone violated me, but He is not angry or disappointed in me because of what happened. Psalm 147:3 assures us, "[The Lord] heals the brokenhearted and binds up their wounds." And after a listing of sins, 1 Corinthians 6:11b says, "But you were washed, you were sanctified, you were justified in the name of the Lord Jesus Christ and by the Spirit of our God."

How reassuring! God made my body in His image. He also heals the broken. When something bad happens, God's promise to me is that He will heal me. Whether I did something wrong or if someone does something to me, He washes and cleans me by the Spirit of God.

Giving Up Control

God has a different idea of control. When we submit to God, He becomes our defender and empowers us to overcome the enemy. James 4:7 charges us to "submit yourselves, then, to God. Resist the devil, and he will flee from you." And 1 Peter 5:6 reminds us to be humble and God will exalt us at the proper time. The previous verse tells us, "God opposes the proud but shows favor to the humble" (1 Peter 5:5b).

Blessings come when we walk in submission to God and in humility with others. And Colossians 3:1 reminds us that submission doesn't humiliate. In fact, it states that God actually raises us up! "Since, then, you have been raised with Christ, set your hearts on things above, where Christ is, seated at the right hand of God." Scripture encourages us to focus on Him in all things. We obey God, who first loved us, because we love Him. Then, as we submit to Him, He doesn't crush us under His feet as a cruel dominator, but lifts us up in His love and blesses us for having humble, obedient hearts.

Humility helps us to understand the truth of the limits of our power and knowledge. I am not alone, and I do not need to figure everything out. God will help direct and guide my path.

Consider all the things you carry—things that worry you. Give them to God. If they are things concerning the future, ask Him for direction. If they are things you are carrying from the past, give those to God and ask His forgiveness for either the sin committed or for trying to bear the burden under your own strength. Then ask Him to free you from those burdens. He is always listening when we speak to Him, and He always wants us to call

Humility

helps us understand the

truth

of our personal

limitations.

out to Him—whether to thank Him for something He's done or to tell Him of a need or fear. He doesn't want us shackled. He wants to bring freedom! Giving up control to Him brings freedom to us.

A Time of Prayer

One of my passions is barrel racing with my horse. A friend and I flew to Texas so I could try a few horses that were more advanced in their training. I wanted to compete at a higher level. We narrowed the search to two horses. The first horse was very sweet and worked well, but needed a bit more work before it would be ready to compete. The other horse was far along and had a real zest for life.

Deciding on a horse was a big financial decision. On our way home, my friend told me to pray about it. I thought that was a good idea and figured I'd pray as soon as I got home. I wanted to make it a serious matter of prayer.

With determination, I got on my knees in front of my couch. I clasped my hands and bowed my head and started praying. I prayed and prayed, but nothing came to me about which horse to choose. I prayed all the words I knew to pray.

As I kneeled there praying, my mind wandered. I studied the fabric on the couch cushion. It was amazing how the manufacturers could weave it together with such precision! I wondered if it was one large piece of fabric that they molded around the sofa, or if they first cut it into sections and sewed it together.

How do they make sure the fabric is the same color? There are so many yards of fabric to make the love seat and sofa, yet they were a perfect color match. How did they do that? They must make tons of these. How do they make sure that the couch and love seat get fabric from the same bolt? How do they keep them together during the manufacturing process to ensure they sold as a set? They must have some type of numbering system so that when they ship, they go to the store together. How does the store ensure they get the matching set to the customers?

Have you ever started out praying with the best intention and then find your mind wandering down rabbit trails that have nothing to do with what you are praying? Praying can happen in times of quiet and solitude when I'm on my knees, but prayer can also happen while I'm busy doing all the everyday things.

Perfect Prayer

The more I talk to God during the day, the closer I feel to Him. When I see something that is beautiful, I often pause and thank Him for His creation. When I need help, I ask Him for direction. If I'm headed to a meeting, I ask God to help me say the right things so that I can do my job well and be helpful to my colleagues.

When I think of a verse from the Bible that fits a decision I need to make, I speak that verse or promise to build my faith as I talk to God. It helps me to remember what God says about things in His Word, because His Word is absolute truth! When I speak scripture back to Him in prayer, His Word says in Isaiah 55 that it will accomplish the purpose for which it was sent! I am not perfect, but the more I pray, the more I see His hand in my life. The more I depend on God, the more peace I feel in every decision I make.

It's reassuring that we can talk to God anywhere. I could have sought His direction while riding the horse or sitting on the plane. We never need to feel we must put on a show for God or pray the perfect words or for a certain amount of time for the prayer to be effective or for Him to hear us. He's always listening! Give Him the reins and then listen to see how He leads you. No matter the situation, God knows the perfect solution.

So is My Word that goes out from My mouth:
It will not return to Me empty,
but will accomplish what I desire
and achieve the purpose for which I sent it.
You will go out in joy and be led forth in peace;
the mountains and hills will burst into song before you,
and all the trees of the field will clap their hands.
Isaiah 55:11-12

CHAPTER 16

Help

Everyone then who hears these words of Mine
and does them will be like a wise man
who built his house on the rock.
And the rain fell, and the floods came,
and the winds blew and beat on that house,
but it did not fall, because it had been founded on the rock.
Matthew 7:24-25, ESV

When I first began dealing with anorexia, losing weight was reinforcing for me. It even became an obsession. I enjoyed having control over my body and I could see the results—my body was wasting away. Anything that impeded progress needed to be removed. I didn't dare tell anyone what I was doing. What would they think of me?

It often frustrated people that I couldn't "just eat." I knew they talked about me behind my back. They thought that if I would just eat, I would be fine. People judged me, and there was no empathy for the disease with which I was dealing. I didn't want pity, but I also didn't choose to have anorexia. It wasn't just hard to eat, it was hard to get up every day and fight the fight.

People who break a leg do not do so on purpose. People battling cancer don't intentionally seek out a pathogen which would make them ill. As a person battling anorexia, it felt like people blamed me for the struggle I faced and often became impatient and frustrated with me. This is difficult for people who are working through eating disorders as they are already under intense anger and frustration with themselves.

People could see how skinny I was, and assumed I was sick, but believed I could just flip a switch and, like magic, everything would be better. For some people, it may work this way. I have heard stories about people who gave their heart to Jesus and He immediately broke the power of an eating disorder over them and they were instantly freed. I believe this can happen. I know Jesus works in amazing ways. My testimony, however, is different.

For me, though the intentions of the people trying to make me eat might have been good, it wasn't helpful. When I woke up, the voice always came flooding in, and it took every ounce of energy I had to get up and face the day.

While the disease was in my head, I could not get myself out of the cycle just by thinking through it. I didn't wake up one morning and decide to torture myself by not eating. It also wasn't productive to have my eating discussed by people around me who didn't understand. Food choices may be easy for them, but they were so hard for me. While I realize they weren't intentionally being rude or hurtful, the enemy surely did try to use the whispers behind cupped hands to wound my heart.

Instead of whispering, it would have been comforting for someone to tell me that they saw how hard this was for me, that they knew I'm struggling. It would have helped to have them say they were available if I needed to talk, or to remind me that I was a wonderful, loved person. They could have asked if they could pray for me or with me, and such words would have come across as non-judgmental and compassionate. Prayer is one of the most powerful weapons we have, after all!

The disease was in my

head,

but I couldn't stop the

cycle of lies

running through it.

The prayer of a righteous person is powerful and effective.
James 5:16b

Patterns

Our minds get used to certain patterns. I can get up in the middle of the night, leave the lights off, walk out of my bedroom, go into the kitchen to get a glass of water, and then walk back to bed—with no lights on to help guide my way. My mind has created a path and I can do this easily because I have done it so many times.

Have you ever moved something and then kept going back to the spot where you used to keep it? One day, my husband moved a little garbage bag I kept in the basement. For four days I went to toss trash in the bag only to find the bag gone. The first time I did it I thought, "Oh yeah, we got rid of that little bag." By the fourth day, I realized I had quite a pattern deep in my mind, and my brain was running on autopilot.

Some people believe it is a simple matter of "just eat" for a person dealing with an eating disorder. It seems obvious to them, but they were not living in my head. I had tried telling myself that when I woke up, I would not worry about food and just eat. I tried to flip the switch. Looking back, I now see how that set me up for failure.

"Flipping the switch" couldn't stop my autopilot pattern of behavior. Instead, my emotions went haywire! It felt like my heart was going to jump out of my body. I couldn't breathe, and it felt like fire was running up and down my arms. I wanted to run as fast as I could, as though I were running from a violent crowd of people intent on harming me.

Doing something out of my usual pattern caused the voice in my head to attack. Not only did I end up not being successful, but I felt worse than before. I was angry and frustrated at my failure. During moments of lucidity, I would even try to trick myself into believing I could eat, or guilt myself into eating. I'd remind myself I was hurting my family and friends. I've even told myself my behaviors were disappointing God.

Breaking the Patterns

Something that worked for me was breaking the pattern slowly. Some of these patterns had been part of my life for so many years that adjusting one or two things a week or a day provided me with better success.

You couldn't take a 16-year-old who's never touched a basketball and throw them into a high school basketball game, expecting a positive experience. Instead, you teach the elements of the game and help them build skills and expertise with the ball. You offer positive reinforcement, knowing skills would need to be developed over time. Coaches spend years training and supporting athletes.

To receive support for an eating disorder, it is best to consult a licensed professional experienced in working with dietitians and medical doctors. Think of these individuals as the coaches. They aren't there to force food down your throat and tell you that makes you better. Skilled professionals are trained to help people navigate recovery.

My therapist shares my belief in the power and love of our Lord Jesus Christ, and used biblical principles on my healing journey. She sees me for who I am and for who God says I am. I can be fully transparent with her. She reminds me I am an amazing woman whom God made and with whom He is pleased.

God saw all that He had made, and it was very good.
Genesis 1:31

We are His creation. He knows you and knows the areas where you are struggling. He does not blame or shame you. God knows your heart and the pain you carry. In 1 Samuel 16:7, the Word says, "But the Lord said to Samuel, 'Do not consider his appearance or his height . . . The Lord does not look at the things people look at. People look at the outward appearance, but the Lord looks at the heart.'"

For by Him all things were created,
in Heaven and on earth, visible and invisible,
whether thrones or dominions or rulers or authorities—
all things were created through Him and for Him.
Colossians 1:16, ESV

God created you, and He loves you. People may not understand the burdens you carry, but God does, and He is willing and able to help. An eating disorder is hard, and it is ok to get help. Seeking a professional to help has been a blessing to me. Just as God gave gifts to you, He also gifted these professionals to help people struggling with eating disorders. They are a safe resource and only want to help free you to fulfill all the good work God has in store for you.

Jesus Christ is the greatest coach, mentor, supporter, and encourager for me. I have only recently begun to understand the power of Jesus and the depths of His love for His children. He has been my rock and my foundation from whom I draw strength and resilience.

I may only have a limited amount of time in the presence of licensed professionals during the week, but I am never alone. I can always call upon the name of Jesus for help and guidance. By looking into the scriptures and stories within the Bible, I can gain insight into the incredible feats He accomplished and the lives He touched. Jesus offered many people strength, encouragement, and guidance, and He enabled them to see a path forward. He can do the same for me and for you!

The Lord is my rock and my fortress and my deliverer,
my God, my rock, in whom I take refuge,
my shield, and the horn of my salvation, my stronghold.
Psalms 18:2, ESV

CHAPTER 17

Get Out of My Head!

You will also decide and decree a thing,
and it will be established for you;
and the light [of God's favor] will shine upon your ways.
Job 22:28, AMP

In Luke 8:26-33, we read about a demon-possessed man. Soldiers had shackled and guarded the man, but the demons in him were so strong he kept breaking the chains and would go wander in the desert (solitary places) by himself.

The man was living alone and naked among the tombs of Gerasa when he met Jesus. Jesus asked the man his name, and he responded "Legion" (meaning many) because there were so many demons inside of him. Jesus commanded the demons out of the man, and they asked Him if He would allow them to enter a herd of pigs nearby. Jesus gave them permission. They entered the pigs, and the pigs drowned in a lake.

I wanted the voice in my head to be gone, too. I wonder what the man called "Legion" felt like after Jesus commanded the demons to leave his body. He might have been in shock! Maybe he was so exhausted he fell at Jesus's feet and slept. Did he get up, dance, sing, celebrate, and praise God? Was he scared the demons would come back? I couldn't imagine being free of the eating disorder voice in my head, but I wanted it gone!

Working Toward Freedom

I imagined all I would do if I were free. How much more time I'd have in my day! I'd run, skip, and dance around in circles to celebrate. When the voice of the eating disorder tried to control my mind, I felt like I was in the middle of an action movie. It was as if two people were fighting back and forth, and the camera angles shift so often that it's hard to get the full picture. Sometimes the scenes are so dark it's difficult to determine who is good or bad.

I want the good guy to win and be free from these demons within me—that part of my consciousness recognizes that truth. Then in a moment, the voice intrudes on my thoughts, telling me lies and manipulating the truth. Sometimes it is loud and clear. Other times, it's quiet and flips things around in my mind so I can't make sense of right and wrong.

If I had a healthy eating plan for the day, the voice would try to come in and hijack it. If I was trying something new, the voice would make me question what I was doing or bring confusion. Was I supposed to start that new eating plan today or next week? My mind would spin while I tried to recall the conversations I'd had with my therapists. If I'd written the plan down, the voice would question the accuracy of what I'd written.

For God is not the author of confusion, but of peace.
1 Corinthians 14:33a, KJV

We have the power to stop demonic influences. The Bible says, "Be alert and of sober mind. Your enemy the devil prowls about like a roaring lion looking for someone to devour. Resist him, standing firm in the faith" (1 Peter 5:8-9a). Paul says in Ephesians 6:12, "For our struggle is not against flesh and blood, but against the rulers, against the authorities, against the powers of this dark world and against the spiritual forces of evil in the heavenly realms."

Another powerful verse says, "For God hath not given us the spirit of fear; but of power, and of love, and of a sound mind." (2 Timothy 1:7, KJV). Other versions of that same verse use the words "self-control" in place of "sound mind," showing our ability to control the things that wonder through our mind and try to stick around. You might not be able to help a thought that pops in, but you can keep it from staying! A supporting scripture for that concept is 2 Corinthians 10:5. It admonishes us to take every thought captive. We shackle our thoughts, not the other way around!

Winning the Argument

When the voice of the eating disorder would speak, I would argue back truth and wisdom. The voice might tell me I didn't need to follow my healthy eating plan, and I would respond with, "Yes, I do." The voice may come back and insist that my old way of doing things worked just fine and suggest I imagine all the bad things that might happen if I followed my counselor's recommendations. It would insist that I would get fat, my clothes would no longer fit, and people would laugh at me. I would respond, "No, that isn't true. I need to stick to my plan because that will make me healthy."

"Yeah, healthy like an ox! Have you ever seen an ox? They're healthy, but they sure are big!" The voice was relentless in attacking my thoughts until my mind would agree, "Oxen are huge and all they do is eat grass. I'm being asked to eat protein. If an ox can be so big only eating grass, what's going to happen to me if I eat

Thoughts may

pop in,

but I can prevent them from

hanging out.

protein? I don't know what to do! I'm scared to follow my plan! I don't want to look like an ox!"

It may sound crazy, but the battle in my mind was non-stop, 365 days a year. We eat three to four times a day. For me, that is over 1,400 conversations about food in a single year. This doesn't even include all the other times the voice invaded my peace and happiness.

Stop

So, when the voice starts, what does "taking your thoughts captive" look like? It looks like a great big red stop sign. I had to learn not to engage when the voice popped up. In the strongest, most confident voice I could muster, I would say, "STOP!" It may try again, and again I would declare, "STOP!"

I have gotten very comfortable saying STOP and laughing at the voices when they try to start a war between my ears. They cannot get me; they cannot hurt me. They have no right in my life, and no right to take away my happiness!

Job 22:28 tells us we will decide and decree a thing, and it will be established for us; and the light (of God's favor) will shine upon our ways (AMP). According to God's Word, I declare I am in charge of my thoughts and God is in charge of my life! Demons, be gone, now, in Jesus' name! I have a sound mind. I have self-control in my thought life, and my thoughts are going to line up with what God says is good for me.

CHAPTER 18

Broken

Casting all your cares [all your anxieties, all your worries,
and all your concerns, once and for all] on Him,
for He cares about you [with deepest affection,
and watches over you very carefully].
1 Peter 5:7, AMP

I once heard a preacher tell a story about a glow stick. He shared about a young mom who was waiting in a long checkout line with two children. Her oldest child had a package of glow sticks, and her toddler was screaming to have one. The mom opened the package and handed the child one of the glow sticks to silence him, and it worked. He was content.

His older brother then took the glow stick away, eliciting screams once again. Before the young mom could correct her older son, he bent the glow stick and gave it back to his sibling. Noticing the stick glowing, the older brother explained it had to be broken to fully enjoy it. Its purpose was always to glow.

As I listened to this story, I felt like leaping for joy! I knew anorexia was not God's plan for my life, but I could hear God saying to my spirit, "I had a greater purpose in allowing you to walk through the hurt and breaking. I created you and gave you promises to hold onto in the dark times. Now it is time to shine and fulfill your purpose."

That precious child was content just swinging that "unbroken" glow stick around in the air because he didn't understand the manufacturer created it to glow. That was how I was, while living with an eating disorder all those years. I was content dealing with my lot in life. While I didn't realize it at the time, God was there all along, willing to help me and leading me through it to my purpose.

God didn't cause me to have anorexia. Anorexia was the plan of the enemy. But God uses what the enemy meant to bring destruction in our lives, to become a personal victory. That victory then becomes, not only a blessing in our life, but allows us to walk others in similar circumstances to their own path of victory when we share His goodness with them. He uses our tragedies to create some of our biggest triumphs.

> The Lord is close to the brokenhearted
> and saves those who are crushed in spirit.
> Psalms 34:18

> You intended to harm me,
> but God intended it for good
> to accomplish what is now being done,
> the saving of many lives.
> Genesis 50:20

The Weight

I carried all the hurt and brokenness with me. I was closed off and weighed with guilt and shame. I had accepted the eating disorder as my destiny. It was something I would always carry around like a backpack loaded with heavy books.

These books held all the "rules" about food—don't snack, never eat chips, don't ever eat until your stomach is full, and only eat at specific times. There were books telling me my identity—you are stupid; you don't know

God uses our

tragedies

to create our biggest

Triumphs.

how to read; you stumble over words when reading aloud because you don't know them. You are an embarrassment. You can't spell, and everything you write has grammatical errors in it. When people see what you write, they think you're dumb and illiterate.

There are other books that defined me as a mother— you don't spend enough time with your kids. You do not cook them good, wholesome meals. You didn't read them enough stories when they were younger. You were too hard on them sometimes and too easy on them at others. How inconsistently you parented! Your children notice all your mistakes, and they don't really love you at all.

There were also books containing pages about my role as a wife—a good wife would cook well, but you don't. You do not keep the house clean. You should wash and iron the clothes. If you were a good wife, you would give up what you're doing and focus on him more. You are so selfish.

The backpack was so heavy it strained my back and shoulders. The books contained all the words anorexia used my whole life to keep me shackled. In my head, I would think, "It's okay. I'm okay. I must keep carrying it." What else could I do? That was all I had known my whole life—make do—be content with the weight. Be content with the way things are. Nothing will ever change. It's impossible.

Perhaps you, too, have been struggling under the weight of the lies of the enemy. He may be whispering, "Be content with what you have. Stop trying to be something you're not. Stop looking ahead. You're never going to get what you hope for. That's never going to happen. There's no point in believing that promise from God's Word. He meant that for somebody else."

The voice of the enemy can start off sounding very close to Scripture. As you continue to give it permission to speak by listening, however, you will find it takes you further from God's plan for your life. God gives us the strength to endure our situations, but also the strength to pursue His greater plan.

> For I have learned to be content
> whatever the circumstances.
> I know what it is to be in need,
> and I know what it is to have plenty.
> I have learned the secret of being content
> in any and every situation,
> whether well fed or hungry,
> whether living in plenty or in want.
> I can do all this through Him who gives me strength.
> Philippians 4:11b-13

True Contentment Loses the Weight

Paul, who wrote the book of Philippians, understood true contentment. God doesn't intend for us to be content with settling for second best. He wants us to follow Him toward His best plan for our lives.

Along the way, no matter the circumstances, Paul kept his focus on Jesus, knowing Jesus would provide everything he needed. Inspired by God, Paul also wrote, "And God is able to bless you abundantly, so that in all things at all times, having all that you need, you will abound in every good work" (2 Corinthians 9:8).

All the lies in the books I'd been carrying had been whispered and shouted in my head by the voice. It always had one goal—to keep me bound and keep my eyes on the problem instead of the One who can set me free and bring true peace, contentment, and provision.

I sought the Lord, and He answered me;
He delivered me from all my fears.
Those who look to Him are radiant;
their faces are never covered with shame.
This poor man called, and the Lord heard him;
He saved him out of all his troubles.
The angel of the Lord encamps around those who fear Him,
and He delivers them.
Taste and see that the Lord is good;
blessed is the one who takes refuge in Him.
Fear the Lord, you His holy people,
for those who fear Him lack nothing.
The lions may grow weak and hungry,
but those who seek the Lord lack no good thing.
Psalms 34:4-10

God never asked me to carry this heavy load. In fact, He's asking me to give it to Him. This guilt, shame, and regret and all the lies I believed that weighed me down so long God wanted me to put down at His feet. As I gave it to Him, I imagined Him lifting it off my shoulders and flinging it beyond the horizon. And just like that, it was gone.

He was always waiting for me to release it to Him—to shift my focus from the problem to the One who is the problem-solver. While the enemy's plan was to keep me

Take your eyes off the

problem

and put your focus
on the One
who is the

problem-solver.

burdened, believing the lies, and feeling all the pain, God had a greater plan in mind. I just needed to trust Him.

I didn't have to be content with my lot in life. I didn't have to accept the plan of the enemy and bondage of anorexia. God wanted me unshackled, glowing from the inside out as I shared with others about the One who made me free.

Trust in the Lord, and do good;
dwell in the land and befriend faithfulness.
Delight yourself in the Lord,
and He will give you the desires of your heart.
Commit your ways to the Lord; trust in Him, and He will act.
Psalms 37:3-5, ESV

CHAPTER 19

Surrounded

Finally, brothers and sisters, whatever is true,
whatever is noble, whatever is right, whatever is pure,
whatever is lovely, whatever is admirable–
if anything is excellent or praiseworthy–
think about such things.
Philippians 4:8

The environment with which we surround ourselves shapes us. I may believe myself to be an independent thinker, but many times what I see and hear around me overshadows or influences my thoughts. Knowing this, I must choose my environment with care, to the best of my ability. I have no control over other people's actions or words, but I can control how I respond and on what I focus.

I'm blessed to work for an amazing company with wonderful people, and I work full time. Most adults spend 40-55 hours each week working and 42-56 hours each week sleeping. This leaves between 57-86 hours each week for adults to fill with a variety of other activities.

What do you do during these hours? Do you spend some of this time watching TV or movies? Are podcasts or reading books more your thing? How much time do you spend scrolling through social media? Are you like so many, who, when they click on the next video reel, they realize they've been viewing video after video for the past two hours? It's an easy trap to which we often fall prey, and you're not alone! I've been there, too.

Time is one thing we never get back, however, so we need to consider how we are spending it, and be selective in what we're watching, reading, or hearing.

Choose Wisely

A friend helped me realize the importance of monitoring my free time better. She was telling me about her choice to adjust what she listened to, what she watched on TV, and what she was reading. She spent her time reading devotionals and reading the Bible. When she watched TV, she watched Christian movies. She spoke in such a positive manner about the impact the change had made in her life that I put aside my initial concerns and tried it.

I was involved in a Bible study at church, and I spent extra time looking up the passages of scripture that were part of the study. I became so engrossed in the lessons that I was sad when the study concluded! The author had written other books, so I purchased one and quickly became absorbed in the new material.

I didn't watch a lot of TV, but when I did, I enjoyed murder mysteries and shows that highlighted criminal investigations. I realized they were affecting my life, because I'd woken up in the middle of the night with nightmares about what I'd seen. My husband had been telling me I needed to stop watching those types of programs, so it was a sign that it was time to adjust what I was feeding my brain in terms of screen time.

I looked for Christian faith-based movies and shows, and found I enjoyed them! I had already been listening to the occasional Christian podcast, but I stopped listening to other podcasts and focused on the ones that would encourage my walk with Jesus. I deleted the apps from my phone that were not in line with my desire to fill my spirit with what was noble, right, pure, admirable, and praiseworthy. Making these adjustments opened the floodgates of the Holy Spirit over me.

So here's what I want you to do, God helping you:
Take your everyday, ordinary life—
your sleeping, eating, going-to-work,
and walking-around life—
and place it before God as an offering.
Embracing what God does for you
is the best thing you can do for Him.
Don't become so well-adjusted to your culture
that you fit into it without even thinking.
Instead, fix your attention on God.
You'll be changed from the inside out.
Readily recognize what He wants from you,
and quickly respond to it.
Unlike the culture around you,
always dragging you down to its level of immaturity,
God brings the best out of you,
develops well-formed maturity in you.
Romans 12:1-2, MSG

The Word of God has shown up in so many ways in my daily life. I feel like God opened my eyes, ears, and heart to experience my relationship with Jesus more fully. I'm also selective with whom I surround myself. I work to strengthen those relationships which are pure, and I spend less time on relationships which are caustic and deteriorate my soul.

Ephesians 5:15 says, "Be very careful, then, how you live—not as unwise but as wise." I want to be a wise steward of my time, so I accomplish all God has planned

Fix your attention on

God.

You'll be

changed

from the inside out.
Romans 12:1b, MSG

for me. We know God's plans by talking with Him and getting in His Word and listening for His directions. He will show us the path to take.

Your Word is a lamp for my feet, a light on my path.
Psalms 119:105

A Healed Fighter

As I continued working on my mind and environment, I also focused on providing my body with the nutrients it needed under the direction of my doctors. My body began to change and people who hadn't seen me in a while sometimes commented on the differences. Their intent was encouragement, but I had to control my mental response to kind-hearted words like, "Wow, you look so good!" My mind would try to revert to the path of distorting the words. I had to speak to myself that when they said, "wow" what they meant was they could see how much I had changed. I had to fight the thoughts that they were implying I had piled on the poundage and should fast-track it to the gym.

Words Have Weight

Some comments were a little harder to digest. I heard, "You're really filling out!" Another comment spoken was, "I'm so happy you've been able to put on some weight. It's so good to see that you're not skinny anymore."

For those who struggle with eating disorders, comments about appearance can trigger and fuel the disorder or cause a relapse. We live in a culture where people perceive weight loss as "good" and weight gain as "bad." This is an imperfect assumption. Weight gain or loss may show a change in health, happiness, or life circumstances, and we don't know which one or why.

When we speak to others, we need to be mindful that not all changes have been easy, and commenting on what we see may not be helpful. Words matter. They can bring life or death to a situation. Proverbs 18:21 says, "The tongue can speak words that bring life or death. Those who love to talk must be ready to accept what it brings" (ERV).

As believers, we must choose to speak life. There is also an added responsibility that our words must be appropriate for the person to whom we are speaking. Scripture charges us to be responsible for what we say, and God holds us accountable for each word. Jesus said in Matthew 12:36, "But I tell you that everyone will have to give account on the day of judgment for every empty word they have spoken." We must choose our words wisely.

Do not let any unwholesome talk come out of your mouths,
but only what is helpful for building others up
according to their needs,
that it may benefit those who listen.
Ephesians 4:29

A Time to Speak and A Time for Silence

I was not powerless. I could choose not to respond to the person and, instead, thank Jesus for setting me free. Recognizing His power in my life helped me to realize those spoken words had no power over me. I focused on the plan to be healthy and enjoy life with Jesus beside me.

There were other times, however, when it was appropriate to respond. While I didn't want to hurt someone who meant well, comments sometimes put me in a position to help a well-meaning person to understand the power their words carried and the effect they might have on others. I would sometimes say, "Conversations about people's weight make me uncomfortable. It is not a measure of someone's worth." Other times, I might say, "Oh, is the weight of other people something you focus on? I am healthy, and that is important to me." Another response I sometimes used was, "I am grateful God gave me this amazing body and through it, I can do good things in this world."

Having a planned response in my back pocket helped me redirect conversations and provide a kind, truthful, loving reply—speaking the truth in love not as an angry retort. It's always better to be a peacekeeper and promise speaker. My health was important, and I wanted to stay free from the lies and control of anorexia.

It's better to be a

peacekeeper

and

promise speaker.

CHAPTER 20

Be Prepared

He who was seated on the throne said,
"I am making everything new!"
Then He said, "Write this down,
for these words are trustworthy and true."
Revelations 21:5

One constant part of being human is change. Our bodies change throughout our lives, and that's nothing to be ashamed of. For those who have been conditioned to think "thin is in" and that weight determines worth, we must flip the script. Weight or size does not define us. We should make finding our worth in who Jesus says we are our goal. I often pray, "God, I am so thankful You are showing me a way through this. I am so grateful I can listen to Your voice—the voice of truth. God, thank You for showing me a new way. Some days may be hard, but You are with me."

New Things

We all go through new seasons in life. There were plenty of changes happening when I got married, for example. I was trying to navigate married life and starting my first job. I knew nothing about being a wife. My parents had a model marriage and made it look so easy! I did not know how hard marriage was going to be.

At 22, I was an independent woman who was in love, sharing a house, finances, and lifestyle with another person. There were so many new experiences for me to figure out, and not all of them were pleasant. Somebody had to clean and take care of the house, and I assumed the traditional wife role. I decorated, cleaned, cooked, washed the windows, and even planted a garden. What

Make finding our

worth

in who

Jesus

says we are

our

goal.

may have looked idyllic to the casual observer was miserable for me.

I had no interest in cleaning. I didn't understand why people washed windows when they were just going to get dirty again. I planted a garden because that's what people did, but then I had to weed it! These things pleased my husband, but they did not please me. I did them because that's what I thought I was supposed to do. The more I took on these traditional tasks, the more I felt like who I was and who I wanted to be was eroding around me. As this feeling of losing myself became stronger, I ate less and worked out more.

Not Skinny Enough

I had started my first career around the time I married, and many of my co-workers were women. Being around a bunch of females was a novel experience. I hadn't been a girly-girl growing up. I didn't play with dolls but had a great time playing chase or riding bikes with the boys in our neighborhood. As I grew, I rode horses, cleaned stalls, bailed hay, and loved the outdoors.

Now I was working in an office. Women who gossiped surrounded me. They degraded one another and tried undermining the work of their colleagues. It was shocking! There were many days I excused myself from our office space and cried in the bathroom. The harder it got, the harder I was on myself.

I slipped back into the patterns of anorexia, but remembering how bad it had been before, I confided in my husband. I didn't want things to get bad again, and knew I needed help.

We got in the car and drove to a behavioral health unit in a nearby town and met with the intake specialist. I explained what was going on and how difficult things were getting for me.

They checked my vitals and my weight. Their diagnosis was that I wasn't that bad and to go home. I was not skinny enough to have an eating disorder.

Finding Help

My husband grew up on a ranch and knew nothing of eating disorders. We decided I would benefit from counseling, and back then, you looked in the Yellow Pages for a counselor. I met a woman who provided counseling out of her home. She was a wonderful lady—kind and empathetic to my situation. We were too embarrassed to use our work insurance which covered mental health, so we selected this woman because we could afford her rate.

This ended up being a three-year dysfunctional process. I know she meant well and maybe her treatment style worked for some people—it just wasn't for me. She hosted the first few meetings in a dark basement room. We talked and did some role-playing. At one point, she was feeding me out of a baby spoon.

I kept going along with her process, thinking there was a deep, dark secret inside of me that needed to be revealed for me to be healed. Her methods didn't sit well with my husband, and he encouraged me to talk to my medical doctor.

She concurred that if we hadn't made progress in the last three years, it may be time to look for alternative treatment. I felt conflicted. I had invested a lot of time with this woman and knew she wanted to help me. I heeded the doctor's advice, however, and met with another woman who took a more behavioral approach to the eating disorder.

Finding New Help

From the moment I met my new counselor, I could tell this was going to be different. It took me a while to trust her, and I struggled to understand how she could make me better if she didn't know the cause of my brokenness or how it had become broken. I remember her saying, "We may never know the why, but we know there is a way forward. We know what we can do today to fight back against the voices of the eating disorder."

For years I'd had a voice in my head telling me lie after lie. As I began to gain trust in my counselor, I opened up about the lie's I'd been told about my worthlessness and inabilities. The voice had eroded my confidence, but my counselor was understanding. She gave me a fresh perspective as she rebutted the lies I'd believed for years, and taught me how to fight back against the lies a day at a time.

It was then that I learned the importance of focusing on the positive things every day. I wrote positive declarations that I could speak over myself each morning and meditate on throughout the day. God considers us so valuable that He allowed His Son to die for our sins. That makes us priceless! I now had a weapon I could use every day to fight the lies of the enemy!

I wrote a section in the back of this book as a resource. There are positive declarations we can speak over ourselves and a passage of scripture to back it up. There is no weapon more important than the Word of God and no voice we believe better than our own, so speak up using the tools God gave to help defeat the enemy! These were the very words that brought me so much freedom.

Making Positive Steps

I also had to learn to avoid scales. In the last 20 years, I have gotten on a scale maybe three times. When a medical professional needs to weigh me, I turn my back. When weight is required for documentation, I've given the same weight from my college days. Scales are a trigger for me. I know this, and I do not want to spend my energy thinking about a number.

Clothes can be another trigger. I remind myself that sizes vary between brands, materials, and designs. Jeans, however, used to be my arch nemesis. I would use them to judge my weight. I tried them on, morning and night, to compare how loose or snug they felt.

As I began my journey to getting healthy, I knew jeans would be a potential problem for me. I talked to my counselor. She said if the clothes don't feel good on you and they become a problem, throw them away. I'd had jeans in my closet for 20 years. They were a measure of where I was with weight. When I decided to kick anorexia to the curb because I wanted a richer life, I tossed all those jeans in the trash. How liberating!

The Gift of Joy

We don't need to be measured! We read in 2 Corinthians 10:12, "For we dare not make ourselves of the number, or compare ourselves with some that commend themselves: but they measuring themselves by themselves, and comparing themselves among themselves, are not wise" (KJV). Comparison is a thief of joy. Joy is a gift from God. It comes from knowing who we are in Christ and being content with our discovery of all He has for us.

> May the God of hope fill you with all joy and peace
> as you trust in Him, so that you may overflow with hope
> by the power of the Holy Spirit.
> Romans 15:13

Finding Grace

When you see a duck gliding smoothly across the surface of a pond, what you don't see is the "underwater" view. You can't see the feet pedaling quickly to keep the duck going in the right direction. Someone with an eating disorder may look calm, cool, and collected on the outside, but may experience turbulence inside. I was thankful to have found an amazing woman to help me during the difficult times. Finding the right help got me going back in the right direction, and I've learned that I don't need to paddle my feet so hard all on my own. I can trust her, and I can trust Jesus.

> Let us then approach God's throne of grace
> with confidence, so that we may receive mercy
> and find grace to help us in our time of need.
> Hebrews 4:16

Comparison

is a

thief

of

joy.

CHAPTER 21

Live the Dream

I will tell you the kind of day I want—a day to set people free.
I want a day that you take the burdens off others.
I want a day when you set troubled people free
and you take the burdens from their shoulders.
Isaiah 58:6, ERV

The enemy may attempt to deceive us by making cruel and inaccurate statements. He attempts to work against what God has planned for us by demeaning us or trapping us in a state of fear.

God crafted a plan for your life and plants dreams in your heart, which correlate with the gifts He has given you. Have you ever had a dream you wanted to chase until it was a reality? What obstacles are stopping you from achieving your goals?

Some dreams are simple, personal desires. There are other dreams that come from deep inside of us—God-planted dreams. These dreams pull at your heart and spur you to get out of bed and get going on them! This book was a God-given dream for me, but for a while, I didn't even realize it.

The thought of talking about my struggles with an eating disorder was inconceivable. Why would I expose myself like that? What would people think? I don't even write well! I was so ashamed of having anorexia that I kept it hidden. I didn't want *anyone* to know, let alone write a book about it.

Over time, I realized the more honest I was with myself and with others about dealing with the disease of anorexia, the more I could expose it and its lies. For a long time, I identified myself as the disease. I *was* Anorexia Sarah. But that is not my name, nor was it who

God created me to be. I am Sarah Rose—victorious child of God.

Hearing the Dream

Anorexia is the enemy. It is something I am fighting. By separating myself from it, I grew stronger. As I did, I kept feeling a pull on my heart, "Tell your story! Tell your story!"

I am not an expert on eating disorders. I am not a medical doctor. Even knowing this, I couldn't deny the still, small voice I was hearing to share my story and about how God helped me. I knew the voice of the eating disorder and the voice of the enemy, and this beckoning and tugging voice was neither!

I argued that I was not an expert about God. I only know what I know. There are far better people to tell others about the goodness and healing power of God. I did not feel qualified! People might criticize and judge me! What if I interpret Scripture differently? Worse yet, what if people use content from my story against me? What if they interrogate me or tease me about eating tuna?

Even when you experience victory in one area of your life, the enemy is always looking for a way to cause us to veer from the path God has for us.

The voice which was prompting and urging me to share how God helped me—that was the voice of God! He planted the dream of writing in my heart so He could get a harvest on the seeds of His divine inspiration. Ephesians 5:26 tells us that He sets us apart and makes us clean "by the washing with water through the Word." His Spirit whispered truths to my heart and mind.

God

plants

dreams in our heart

so He can get a

harvest

on seeds

of divine inspiration

watered

by His Word.

Everyone has a story, and this story is mine. It is right to share, and He assured me He would be with me through the process—just as He helped me fight anorexia. The Lord told me He wouldn't put it on my heart if it wasn't something He created me to do.

God's Call

God calls us. Will we answer or talk ourselves out of His command? You have something special to bring to the world. It could be a tug on your heart to speak to someone you see. Don't listen to the lie, "they might not like me or think I'm crazy." When God calls you to do something, do it! As you fill your heart with His Word and protect it from the lies of the enemy, you will find He will call you to even more!

> Above all else, guard your heart,
> for everything you do flows from it.
> Proverbs 4:23

Shine

The enemy loves to stomp out our dreams using fear of failure or rejection. God wants you to shine. He wants you to tell others of His goodness and faithfulness in times of trial and of His presence in times of struggle and victory. Matthew 5:16 says, "In the same way, let your light shine before others, that they may see your good deeds and glorify your Father in Heaven." God wants to use us to be the light of Jesus to those around us. We may not have the answers for which they are searching, but we can point them to the One who does! God has already given you the gifts you need to shine brightly for Him.

Each of you should use whatever gift you have received
to serve others,
as faithful stewards of God's grace in its various forms.
If anyone speaks, they should do so
as one who speaks the very words of God.
If anyone serves,
they should do so with the strength God provides,
so that in all things, God may be praised
through Jesus Christ.
To Him be the glory and the power for ever and ever.
Amen.
1 Peter 4:10-11

Use the gifts He has put inside you, and for each thing He has called you to do, do it with all your might. Colossians 3:23-24 tells us, "Whatever you do, work heartily, as for the Lord and not for men, knowing that from the Lord you will receive the inheritance as your reward. You are serving the Lord Christ" (ESV). When you are walking out the things God has asked you to do, those God-dreams He planted in your heart, complete the task with all you have. Give it your very best. If the Lord has called you to it, He will guide you through it, and it is for a greater purpose than you can imagine. He sees every person your life will touch, and He always has the bigger plan in mind.

When it gets hard, we can ask God to fight for us. Matthew 7:7 says, "Ask and it will be given to you; seek and you will find; knock and the door will be opened to you." The enemy may try to trick us, but we can use the truth of God's Word to shut him down, just like Jesus did. We can remember the ways God has helped us before and remember He hasn't changed. He is still available to help us when we need Him. Jesus wants us to be a light for Him to those around us. Our focus is to obey God's commands, use the gifts He's given us already, and shine brightly as we point others to Jesus. That is living the dream.

CHAPTER 22

The Way Forward

God has chosen you and made you His holy people.
He loves you.
So your new life should be like this: show mercy to others.
Be kind, humble, gentle, and patient.
Don't be angry with each other, but forgive each other.
If you feel someone has wronged you, forgive them.
Forgive others because the Lord forgave you.
Together with these things, the most important part
of your new life is to love each other.
Love is what holds everything together in perfect unity.
Let the peace that Christ gives control your thinking.
It is for peace that you were chosen to be together
in one body.
And always be thankful.
Colossians 3:12-15, ERV

I've had the voice of the eating disorder chirping in my ear, saying negative things to me for 30 years. It is hard to look at myself without anorexia pointing out some flaw or imperfection to manipulate my feelings. It wants to bring shame and keep me shackled. This voice belongs to the enemy, trying to keep me from the joy of God. I hope that, in sharing my story, others can see there is a way out.

My counselor has been working with me on learning to take a compliment. When someone says something nice to me, I struggle to receive and believe it. I am very hard on myself and want to be perfect. Because this is my natural tendency, it is easier to look at the things I do not do well.

A performance review from my job once read, "On personal development, I believe you would benefit from continuing to focus on being gentle with yourself and gentle with others. As I have said before, I sometimes hear you say strong, negative words, generally about yourself, but sometimes in conversation toward others. Improving your 'self-talk' increases your resiliency in hard times." My boss read this review aloud to me. Written in black and white, the review devastated me. The person who completed the review asked, in the kindest way possible, "what can I do to help?"

I looked across the table, trembling inside and wanting to break down in tears and tell them my life story. The most hurtful part of the review regarded my being gentle to others. Knowing that my words hurt other people was crushing. I wanted them to know I was having a hard time, but I was doing the best I could. Instead, I just said I didn't know.

Learning Love

It's hard to love others if you do not love yourself. I think for many of us, learning to love ourselves is a constant journey. We never finish learning to love, but we have to start somewhere.

Loving yourself doesn't happen overnight, but it begins with a thankful heart. In the mornings, I thank God for the rest I've had and the ability to rise. I thank Him for all the beautiful creation around us and that He created my body to feel the cold air outside and the warmth of the house. I'm thankful to smell the fresh cut grass and a lit candle. These little things are important, because these are beautiful things our body does for us. As I think about myself, I think about every part of me and of myself as a whole. God created me beautifully.

I praise You because I am fearfully and wonderfully made;
Your works are wonderful, I know that full well.
Psalms 139:14

Who Am I

I'm a woman who brought a life into this world. I've traveled halfway around the world to bring home a son from Africa. I have looked through the lens of a camera and captured the beauty in the world I see. I work tirelessly to take care of those around me.

I'm a woman who wraps her arms around a horse with joy. I thoughtfully craft messages to those I love. I've got lines on my face from smiling at my children and I work to build a home for my family. I'm fierce—I will fight for the needs of my husband and children. I'm brave—willing to risk criticism and judgment to share a story to help others. Who are you?

I feel at my best when I'm surrounded by positive, pure, godly things. With what are you surrounding yourself? Who are the people you call friends? Are they positive? Do they encourage and bring joy to your life? What do you watch on TV or consume on your phone? Do those things really bring you joy? Do they draw you closer to Jesus? Do they reinforce the person God created you to be?

When is the last time you did something nice for yourself or for someone else? Something as simple as a little catnap in the sunshine on a Saturday afternoon is a beautiful gift I give myself. It gives my mind a chance to slow down, gaze out of the window, cuddle my dog, and reflect on the goodness of God in my life. I can take time to give my children an extra hug and soak up the moment. I can take a bath, light a candle, or find a special place to be alone with my thoughts and just rest.

I Am Loved

We all are beautiful, and God loves each one of us just the way we are. I recently went to one of those classes where everyone gets a canvas to paint a picture. There were 25-30 people with a variety of skill levels with whom the teacher was working. It was an hour and a half class, and I could hear the conversations around the room.

One thing that stood out to me was how critical everyone was of their own work. I got up and walked around the class and looked at the unique pictures. Each was wonderful! I wonder if that's how God feels, looking down at each of us. Sometimes we're sitting down here being critical of His work and as He looks down upon us, He sees His creation—beautifully and wonderfully made.

Resiliency

There are days where it never crosses my mind I *had* an eating disorder. Other days, that pesky little voice intrudes into my thoughts. When it does, I need to be ready to fight!

We must be resilient. I used to hate that word. I didn't want to keep being resilient. Hadn't I taken enough punches already? There have been times I felt like I was down for the count, and resilient was the last word I wanted to hear.

You are a

beautiful,

wonderful,

loved,

and

unique

creation of

God.

Do not rejoice over me [amid my tragedies],
O my enemy!
Though I fall, I will rise;
Though I sit in the darkness [of distress],
the Lord is a light for me.
Micah 7:8, AMP

But we are resilient. I can spring back up and be ready to fight when needed. I can stand toe to toe with the enemy when those voices come in and punch them out before they touch me. Then I put the enemy back under my feet where he belongs.

Stand

After all the progress I have made, you'd think I'd be standing on stable ground. My days must be so much easier after conquering so much. Surely, I can send the enemy away every time he tries to trick me.

But I still get stuck from time to time. It happens most often when I have done something I regret. I look back at my behavior and feel sad about my actions, and the enemy tries to take that feeling and turn it into shame. I try to suppress the emotions and move away from God, falsely thinking I'll feel better. The enemy then tempts me with the eating disorder and whispers lies to make me question God's love for me. When I listen, I begin to believe and succumb to the lies.

This is why spending time in God's Word, talking to Him, and coming clean when I've messed up is so important. Moving away from God is never the right answer. Seeking His forgiveness for my mistakes is.

We must always remember who He says we are. The Word is full of promises we can trust to bring the breakthroughs for which we believe. It is also full of reminders of His love for us and who He created us to be. We can dig into the Word to get His wisdom for conquering the enemy and reassuring us of who we are in Him. His Word is the truth. Anything else we hear that is contrary to His Word is a lie.

Deuteronomy 30:19 says, "This day I call the heavens and the earth as witnesses against you that I have set before you life and death, blessings and curses. Now choose life, so that you and your children may live."

In this passage, we are reminded that we always have a choice. We can choose to believe the lies (which lead to death) or believe the truth (which leads to freedom and blessings). The choice is ours, but God's Word tells us the right choice to make. Choose life!

I choose to believe life-filled words. I am a powerful warrior of our Lord in Jesus Christ. Each day I reach out to Him for strength and direction. I recognize God as a gentle, kind, loving Father who wants to nourish me with His Word. I know He wants to provide guidance and direction when I get lost. The Holy Spirit comforts me when I stumble so I can get up and try again. God will not strike me down with a bolt of lightning or shower bad things into my life as punishment. He is too good a Father for that.

Instead, He will pick me up and show me a better way. I can fight with the weapons my Savior gave me! I can stand up and speak Truth back and conquer the lies of the enemy.

God knew I would have times where I'd stumble. We all do! And that is why God sent His only begotten Son down to earth to be human like us and to die for our sins. That gift enables me to ask God for forgiveness and receive His freedom so I can withstand the enemy's attempts to make me stumble and move on to do glorious works in His name.

Finally, be strong in the Lord and in His mighty power.
Put on the full armor of God,
so that you can take your stand against the devil's schemes.
For our struggle is not against flesh and blood,
but against the rulers, against the authorities,
against the powers of this dark world and against the
spiritual forces of evil in the heavenly realms.
Therefore put on the full armor of God,
so when the day of evil comes,
you may be able to stand your ground,
and after you have done everything, to stand.
Ephesians 6:10-13

I want to leave you with hope. In life, there are dark and scary days. There are sad and discouraging days. But there are also days so full of joy and freedom! The future is full of glorious experiences waiting for us to get there, so let go of the past and step into your future!

CHAPTER 23

Fearless

Strength and dignity are her clothing
and her position is strong and secure;
and she smiles at the future
[knowing that she and her family are prepared].
Proverbs 31:25, AMP

It was a warm winter's day. A light coat of snow covered the ground. It was time for some fresh air, so I took my dog for a walk on the ice-covered lake. I listened to the sounds of nature, observing how God provided such beauty, even on cold winter days.

My little dog was walking, running, and jumping in the snow about ten feet in front of me as we began, but the farther we went, the more he slowed. I looked down at the path he made.

When he was walking, there were only two imprints of his little feet in the snow—he was tracking perfectly. The front foot would make an impression, the back foot would land precisely on that spot. I was marveling at this, knowing that if I turned around and tried to walk in my exact tracks back to the house, it would be nearly impossible.

Then he started looking on either side of him—perhaps looking for movement or bunnies he could chase. When his head moved right and left, the tracks in the snow were no longer precise. When he focused his attention straight ahead, his steps would immediately line back up again.

Trust in the Lord with all your heart
and lean not on your own understanding;
in all your ways submit to Him,
and He will make your paths straight.
Proverbs 3:5-6

Reflections

As I reflected on what I was seeing, it reminded me of myself. When I fix my eyes and focus on what is ahead, following Jesus, my path is straight. I stay in line with where He wants me to place my feet. When I get distracted by listening to the voice of anorexia or focus on those around me, I end up off-course.

Recovering from an eating disorder is a journey. If you take it one step at a time and focus on the truth and hope Jesus provides, you will find the journey easier to navigate. There are times I was tempted to succumb to the influence of the enemy. But I had the strength to overpower that temptation when I kept my focus on the Word of God and asked Him to direct my steps as I navigated the difficult terrain.

In Matthew 14, the Word records the story of Jesus feeding the five thousand with five loaves of bread and two fish. After that miracle, Jesus sent the disciples on a boat ahead of Him while He went up a mountainside alone to pray. The wind was against the boat, and verse 24 explains it was being, "tossed and battered by the waves" (AMP).

Then here comes Jesus, walking on the water toward them in the early hours of the morning—except they thought it was a ghost! They cried out in fear, "But immediately He (Jesus) spoke to them, saying, 'Take courage, it is I! Do not be afraid!'" (Matthew 14:27, AMP). Peter responded that if it was really Jesus, for Him to command Peter to come to Him.

What a brave thought that was! Peter may have meant to test the identity of Jesus, but he had enough faith to understand Jesus had authority over a turbulent sea. After all, he had already witnessed Jesus speak to a storm and cause the wind and waves to still (Matthew 8:23-27).

Jesus commanded Peter to come to Him. Matthew 14:29b-33 says:

> Then Peter got down out of the boat, walked on the water and came toward Jesus. But when he saw the wind, he was afraid and, beginning to sink, cried out, "Lord, save me!" Immediately Jesus reached out His hand and caught him. "You of little faith," He said, "why did you doubt?" And when they climbed into the boat, the wind died down. Then those who were in the boat worshiped Him, saying, "Truly You are the Son of God."

Peter was bold enough to step out of the boat, but when he let his eyes focus on his environment instead of focusing on Jesus, he got off track. When Jesus calls us to do something, that is not the time to get distracted. A successful walk with Jesus requires obedience and focus.

Focus in Faith

My journey has been long, with many twists and turns. I've struggled and I've recovered. I've been in a process. There have been moments of success and moments of failure. I know what it is to feel the trials of a storm and the feeling of being battered by the waves, my life as fragile as a small boat on an enormous sea.

A successful walk with Jesus

requires

obedience

and

focus.

Jesus's commands, however, are to not doubt and not be afraid. The turbulent waters of anorexia may surround me, and I may feel I'm tumbling. The enemy may shout my failures in my head and try to get me to turn from the knowledge of who God created me to be. When that happens, I must remember Jesus has authority over the wind and waves.

He's also given me that same authority over the enemy, and I have the Word of God to slice lies to the ground. He's given that authority to you, too. We must always remember who we are and whose we are. We are His. We are loved with an unfathomable love and have the power to walk in victory and to bring others along with us.

Like the Proverbs 31 woman, we are strong and secure in our position as children of God, and we can smile (and even laugh) at the future, because we are prepared for it. He has given us everything we need for a life of fulfillment, joy, peace, success, and freedom. Freedom awaits us! We can silence the lies and choose to walk into the purpose and plan God has for our future. We are not alone. God is with us! As we focus in faith on the power of God and the promises in His Word, we can be fearlessly unshackled.

Acknowledgements

Mary Ellen Smith, you saved my life. You made me recognize that the eating disorder was the enemy. You showed me how it deceived me and kept me from all the amazing things God had planned for my life. I'm thankful for your truthfulness and assistance to rediscover the voice of God.

Dr. Debra Rodeghiero Johnston, I am deeply appreciative of your support over the last 20 years. You've always treated me with grace and kindness. You have the courage to ask challenging questions and strive to understand everything I have gone through while giving me the best treatment options.

Holly Murray, when I asked God to help direct me in writing this book, I didn't know what to expect. I had to be brave and fully transparent about my journey, exposing the deepest part of myself so others would know the great power of Jesus. It was a divine appointment that God brought you into my life when He did. From the first time we spoke, I could hear God speaking through you. I really don't know how I was so blessed to find you and for you to agree to help me tell my story. All I can say is that it was God's plan. Holly, you're an amazing woman of God. Thank you for sharing your gifts with me.

To my family - You all have seen the worst of me and the best of me. I am sorry for the burden and concern you have carried over the years. By sharing my story, I hope others will find hope and healing.

About the Author

In first grade, Sarah displayed difficulty learning. She was held back that year, but it took ten more years before she was identified as having dyslexia. She was pulled from her classes and sent to separate classrooms to learn how to deal with the learning disabilities. Using some self-taught techniques, she went on to overcome the learning disabilities, and received her BS and MBA.

She struggled with body image issues early in life, and in high school, was diagnosed with anorexia. Sarah struggled with the disease for 30 years. With the support of family, friends, and great counselors and physicians, she made significant steps in her health. She learned that whatever the enemy threw at her, God empowered her to conquer through the power of the name of Jesus and the authority He has given.

After college, Sarah married. She and her husband Todd have been married over two and a half decades. They struggled trying to conceive, and just when they accepted it wasn't meant to be for them, she got pregnant and had their first son, Hunter.

Sarah and Todd longed for more children, and God tugged at their heart to adopt. They adopted their second son, Don, from the Democratic Republic of Congo when he was five years old.

Twelve months after the adoption was finalized, Sarah was diagnosed with ovarian cancer. Though the diagnosis and treatment were scary, she had peace from

God through the process. He brought healing to her body, and she is now cancer-free.

Despite the struggles Sarah has faced in life, she is determined. She has managed not only to have survived, but has become someone who brings hope to those around her. She motivates and inspires readers everywhere not to focus on impossibilities, but instead, to find ways to make the possible happen.

Sarah is always looking for ways to make changes, uncover a better plan, and embrace new challenges. She advocates for the rights of those who have been silenced and oppressed. She believes no one should be discriminated against or persecuted for any reason.

Sarah loves running fast horses, capturing beauty from the lens of a camera, making something out of seemingly nothing, and sharing her love for God with others. She is a mother, wife, daughter, sister, and a friend. She is a survivor, and her life serves as a reminder of the healing power of God.

You can learn more and connect with Sarah on her website www.sarahannrose.com. She would love to hear from you!

Created as the *perfect companion*

- ✸ 365 days of positive confessions

- ✸ Daily focus scripture

- ✸ Journaling prompts to help you:

    - ✸ express daily gratitude

    - ✸ focus on what God is saying today

    - ✸ choose self love over loathing

    - ✸ write daily reflections to track growth

Thank You

Thank you for purchasing and reading *Fearlessly Unshackled*. My goal in writing was to help one person, and this goal required transparency. Through the vulnerability of writing my story, I pray you or someone you love and care about is touched. I also pray God's richest blessings over your life and that you recognize His love for you.

If you liked what you read, please take a moment to leave a review online. I'd love to hear your feedback on how this book affected your life! Also, be sure to share your recommendation of *Fearlessly Unshackled* with others. Your review and recommendation help others decide if this book will benefit them. Your voice counts, and I appreciate it!

Blessings,

Rose

Sarah Ann Rose

Declarations

The Word of God is a powerful weapon God gave us. The positive declarations listed in this section are scripturally sound, and a great way to feed your mind as you speak them aloud over yourself each day. This is who God says you are, so proclaim them with boldness!

For more declarations, check out Sarah's journal *Choosing Life: A 365 Day Journal of Positive Scriptural Declarations for Overcoming Eating Disorders*. It is designed to accompany this book and help renew the mind and establish a personalized, healthy nourishment plan every day for a year. Available on Amazon.

I am loved.

For I am convinced that neither death nor life,
neither angels nor demons,
neither the present nor the future, nor any powers,
neither height nor depth, nor anything else in all creation,
will be able to separate us from the love of God
that is in Christ Jesus our Lord.
Romans 8:38-39

I am God's creation.

For You created my inmost being;
You knit me together in my mother's womb.
I praise You because I am fearfully and wonderfully made;
Your works are wonderful, I know that full well.
Psalms 139:13-14

I can face anything.

You, dear children, are from God and have overcome them,
because the One who is in you
is greater than the one who is in the world.
1 John 4:4

I am valuable.

Your beauty should not come from outward adornment,
such as elaborate hairstyles and the wearing of gold jewelry
or fine clothes. Rather, it should be that of your inner self,
the unfading beauty of a gentle and quiet spirit,
which is of great worth in God's sight.
1 Peter 3:3-4

I honor God with my body.

Do you not know that your bodies are temples
of the Holy Spirit, who is in you,
whom you have received from God?
You are not your own; you were bought at a price.
Therefore honor God with your bodies.
1 Corinthians 6:19-20

I make great choices and am pleasing to God. He knows my heart.

The Lord does not look at the things people look at.
People look at the outward appearance,
but the Lord looks at the heart."
1 Samuel 16:7b

I trust God to lead my every step.

Since You are my rock and my fortress,
for the sake of Your name, lead and guide me.
Psalm 31:3.

I am victorious.

Who is it that overcomes the world?
Only the one who believes that Jesus is the Son of God.
1 John 5:5

I am strong and courageous.

Be strong and courageous.
Do not be afraid or terrified because of them,
for the Lord your God goes with you;
He will never leave you nor forsake you.
Deuteronomy 31:6

God is with me, I will not fear.

The Lord Himself goes before you and will be with you;
He will never leave you nor forsake you.
Do not be afraid; do not be discouraged.
Deuteronomy 31:8

I can do anything with God.

I can do all things through Him who gives me strength.
Philippians 4:13

I trust God's plan for my life.

Therefore I tell you, do not worry about your life,
what you will eat or drink; or about your body,
what you will wear. Is not life more than food,
and the body more than clothes?
Matthew 6:25

I am protected.

Even though I walk through the darkest valley,
I will fear no evil, for You are with me;
Your rod and Your staff, they comfort me.
Psalms 23:4

I choose friends who will be good for me.

Walk with the wise and become wise,
for a companion of fools suffers harm.
Proverbs 13:20

God will never fail or abandon me.

And I will ask the Father,
and He will give you another advocate
to help you and be with you forever.
John 14:16

God gives me strength to stick to my plan.

May the God who gives endurance and encouragement
give you the same attitude of mind toward each other
that Christ Jesus had.
Romans 15:5

Resources

Altrogge, M. (2017, April 20). What does it mean to fear god? Biblestudytools.com. Retrieved February 6, 2023, from https://www.biblestudytools.com/bible-study/topical-studies/what-does-it-mean-to-fear-god.html

Anorexia nervosa. Adolescent Growth. (n.d.). Retrieved January 22, 2023, from https://adolescentgrowth.com/treatment-programs/eating-disorders/anorexia-nervosa/

Eating disorder statistics: General & Diversity stats: Anad. National Association of Anorexia Nervosa and Associated Disorders. (n.d.). Retrieved January 21, 2023, from https://anad.org/eating-disorders-statistics

Espíndola, C., & Blay, S. (2009, February 19). Anorexia nervosa's meaning to patients: a qualitative synthesis. *Psychopathology, 42*(2), 69-80. https://doi.org/10.1159/000203339

G342. (n.d.). anakainosis. Strong's Greek Lexicon (KJV). Retrieved June 17, 2023, from https://www.blueletterbible.org/lexicon/g342/kjv/tr/0-1

Jaramillo, S. (n.d.). *What is the Ed Voice and how do I shut it up!* Peace & Nutrition™. Retrieved January 28, 2023, from https://peaceandnutrition.com/what-is-the-ed-voice-and-how-do-i-shut-it-up

Mayo Foundation for Medical Education and Research. (2018, February 20). *Anorexia nervosa*. Mayo Clinic. Retrieved February 2, 2023, from https://www.mayoclinic.org/diseases-conditions/anorexia-nervosa/diagnosis-treatment-drc-20353597

Mayo Foundation for Medical Education and Research. (2018, February 20). *Anorexia nervosa*. Mayo Clinic. Retrieved January 21, 2023, from https://www.mayoclinic.org/diseases-conditions/anorexia-nervosa/symptoms-causes/syc-20353591

NEDA. (2022). *Toolkits*. National Eating Disorders Association. Retrieved January 21, 2023, from https://www.nationaleatingdisorders.org/toolkits

Pugh, M. (2020). Understanding 'ed': A theoretical and empirical review of the internal eating disorder 'voice.' *Psychotherapy Section Review, 1*(65), 12-23. https://doi.org/10.53841/bpspsr.2020.1.65.12

Pugh, M. and Waller, G. (2016). The anorexic voice and severity of eating pathology in anorexia nervosa. *International Journal of Eating Disorders.* https://doi.org/10.1002/eat.22499

Silén, Y., & Keski-Rahkonen, A. (2022, November 1). Worldwide prevalence of DSM-5 eating disorders among young people. *Current Opinion in Psychiatry, 35*(6), 362-371. https://doi.org/10.1097/YCO.0000000000000818

Thornton, C. (2021, June 11). *The eating disorder voice*. The Redleaf Practice. Retrieved January 28,2023, from https://theredleafpractice.com/the-eating-disorder-voice

What is recovery? National Association of Anorexia Nervosa and Associated Disorders. (n.d.). Retrieved

January 27, 2023, from https://anad.org/get-informed/what-is-recovery

Zavada, J. (2019, July 3). *Meet Caleb: A Man who Followed God Wholeheartedly*. Learn Religions. Retrieved January 21, 2023, from https://www.learnreligions.com/caleb-followed-the-lord-wholeheartedly-701181

Launch Team

A special thanks goes out to the team of people who have worked so hard to help share about this book with others. Your encouraging words have kept me focused on why God called me to write. I pray God blesses you abundantly for the time and energy you spent helping me with this project!

Kimberly Aiken
Camille Babin
Stephanie Bohlen
RaeAnn Bowes
Christina Brazell
Tanika Brown
Carmen Davis
Nicchole Dey-Foy
Wendy Duncan
Ashley Falkenhagen
Kira Hill
Ashley Horsch-Hewitt
Martha Jackson
Terri Judy

Rhonda Lyons
Bruni Martinez
Sara McGee
Laura Overbo
Leslie Pierson
Brooke Rollag
Todd Rose
Kelly Jo Scofield
Star Smith
Holly Thomas
Denise Van Plew
Betty Youngblood
Theresa Zimmerman